This Coloring Book Belongs to:

....

Date:

....

Some graphic elements in this book have been created by Drawnhy97, Doodle_flower, Onfocus, GarryKillian, Rawpixel.com, Pikisuperstar at Freepik.com

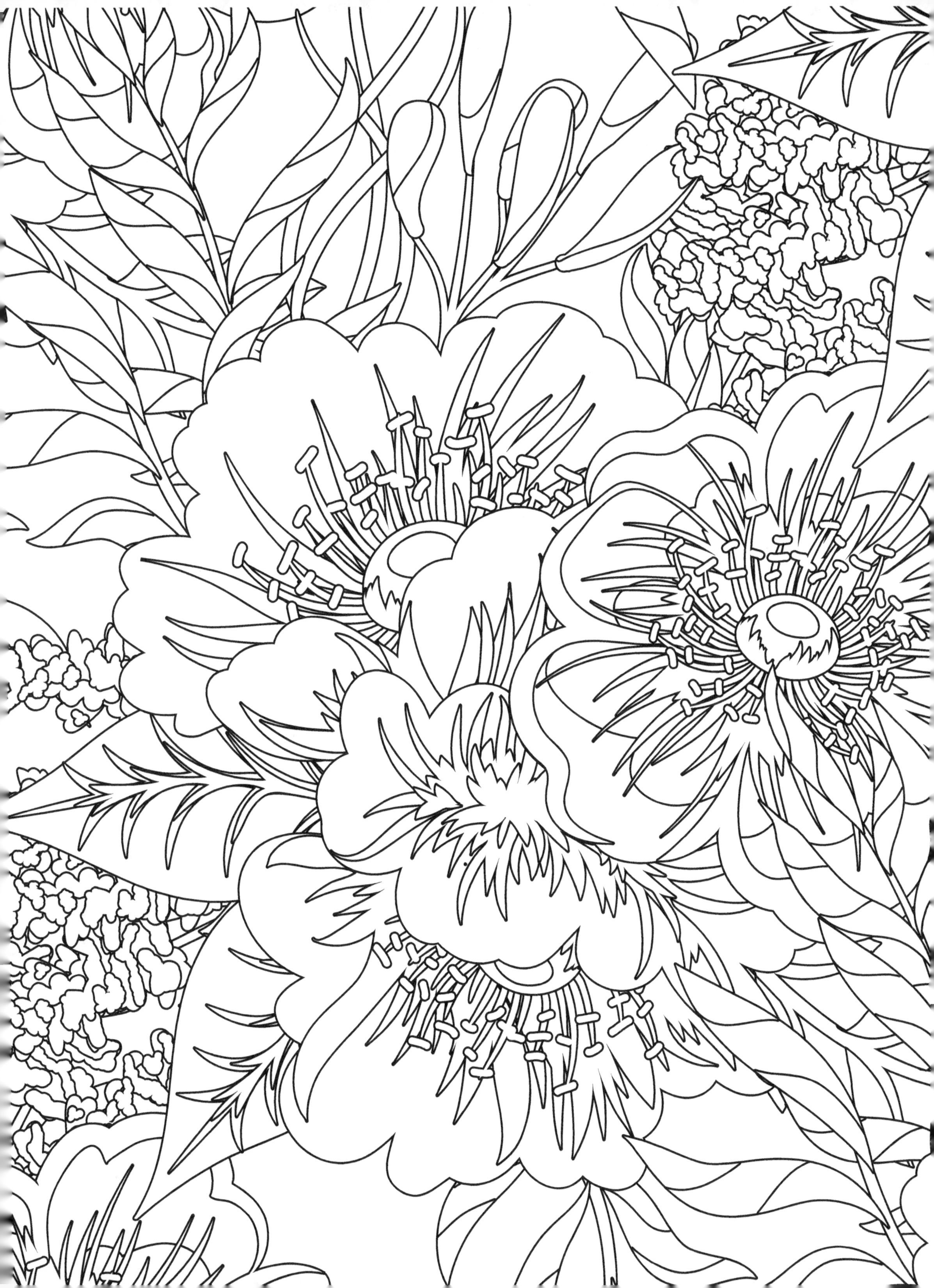

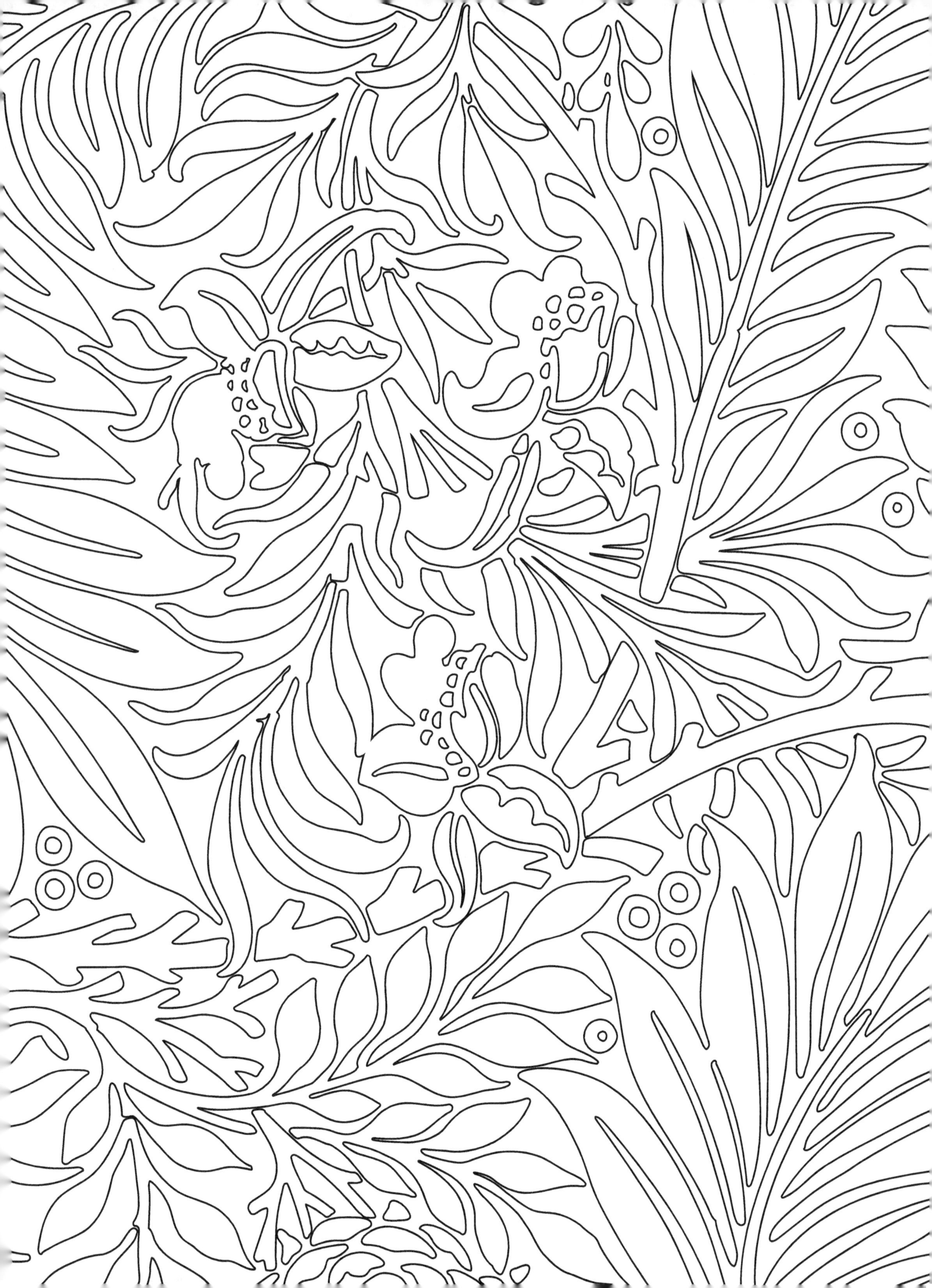

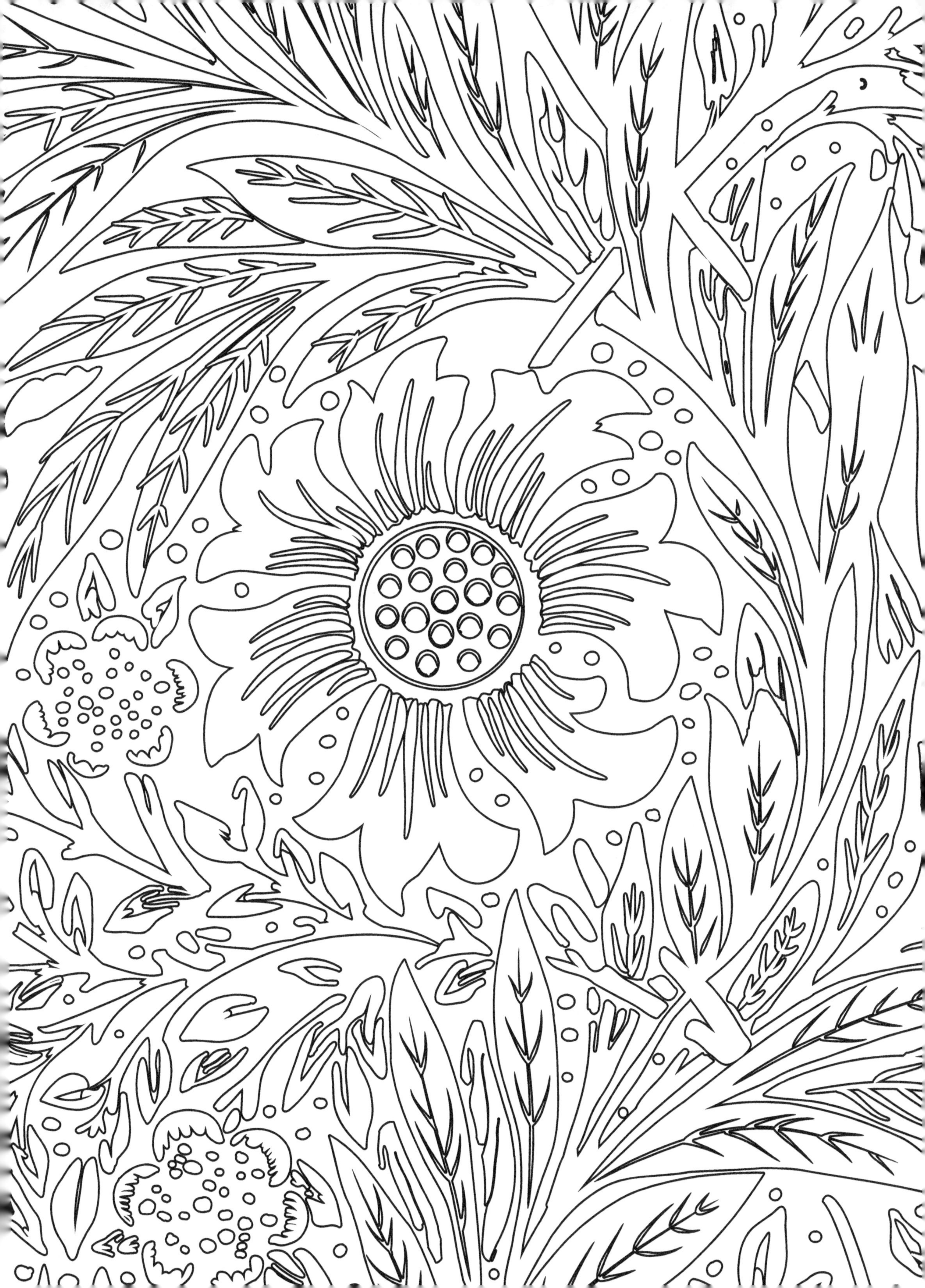

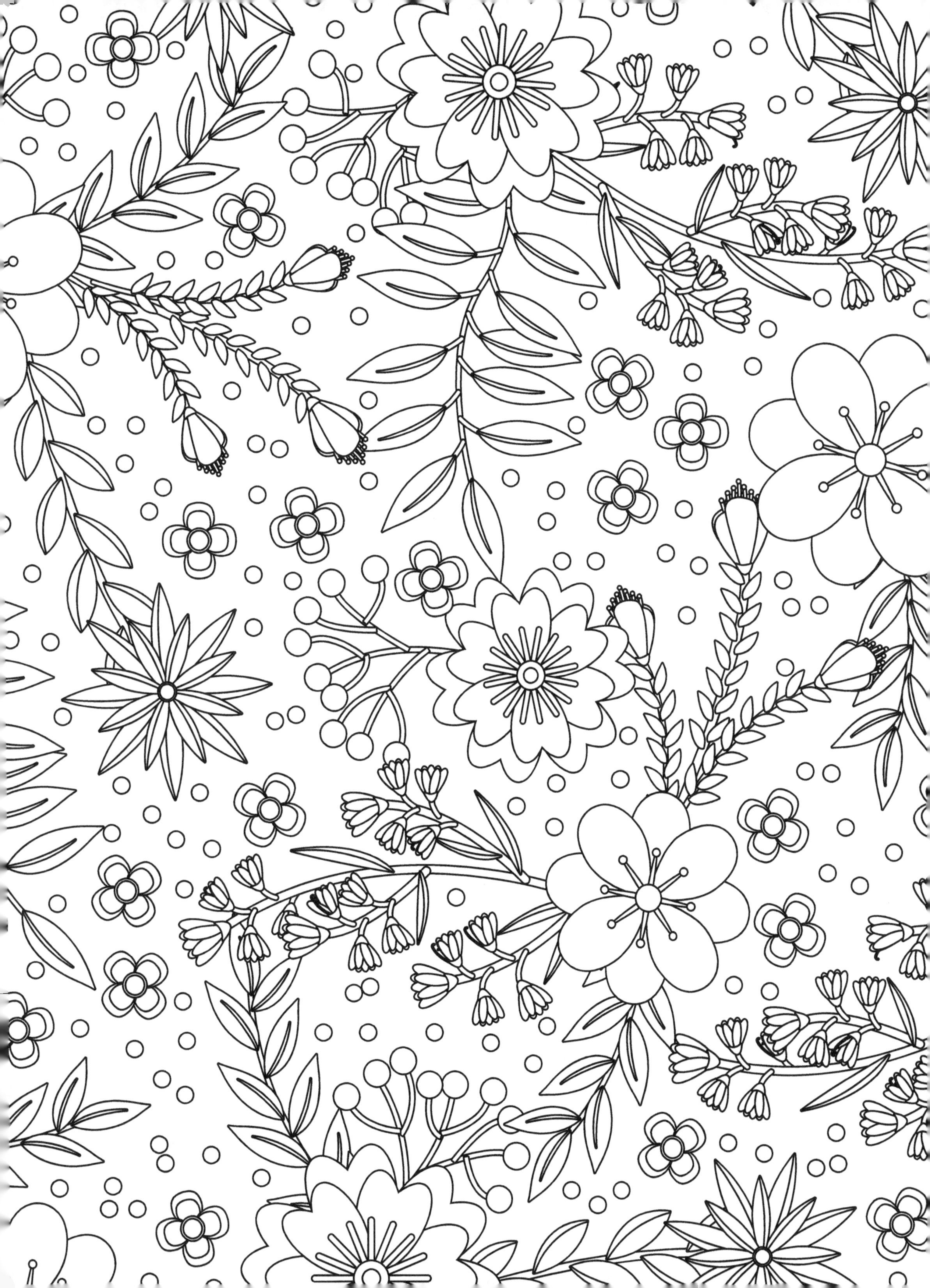

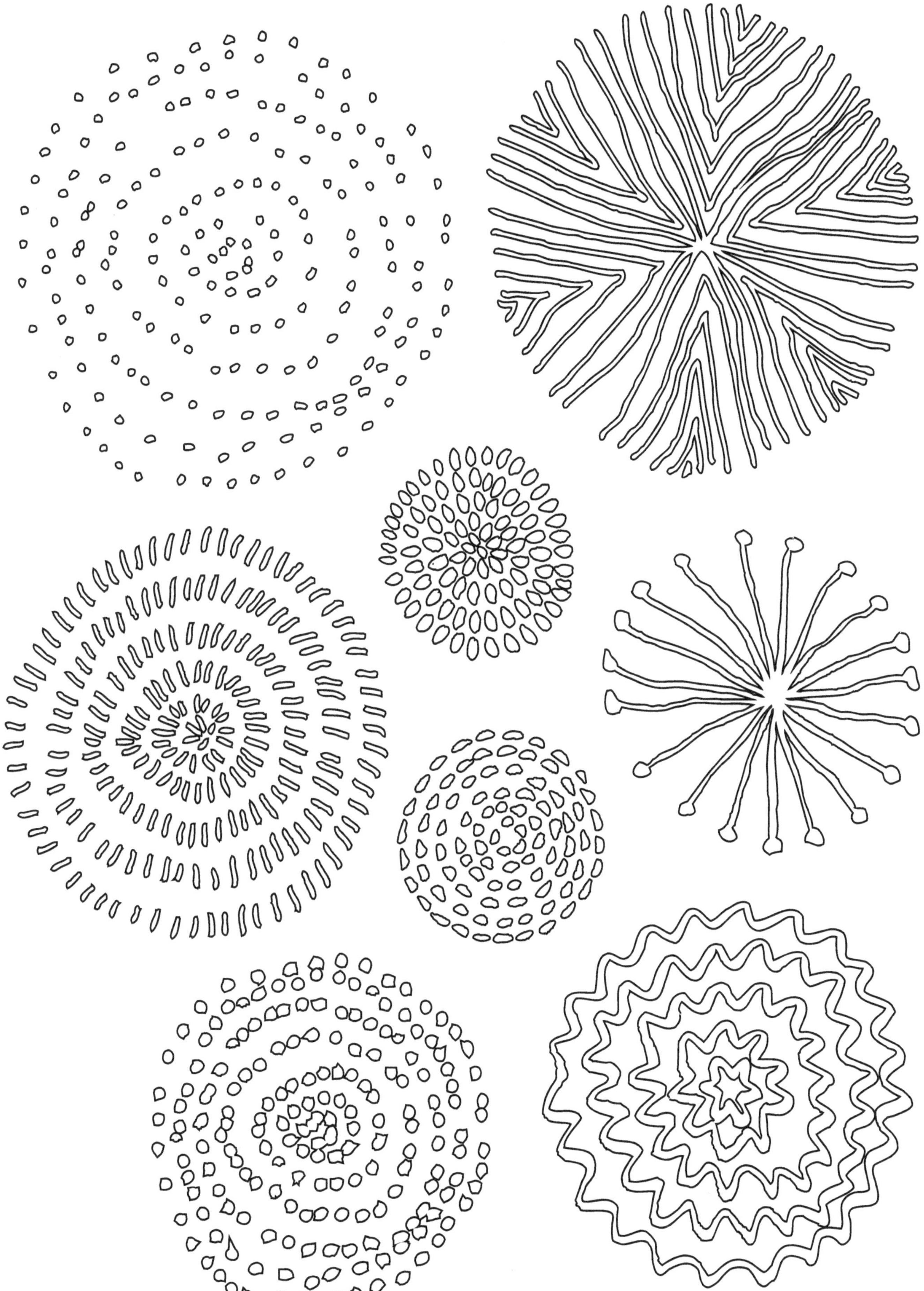

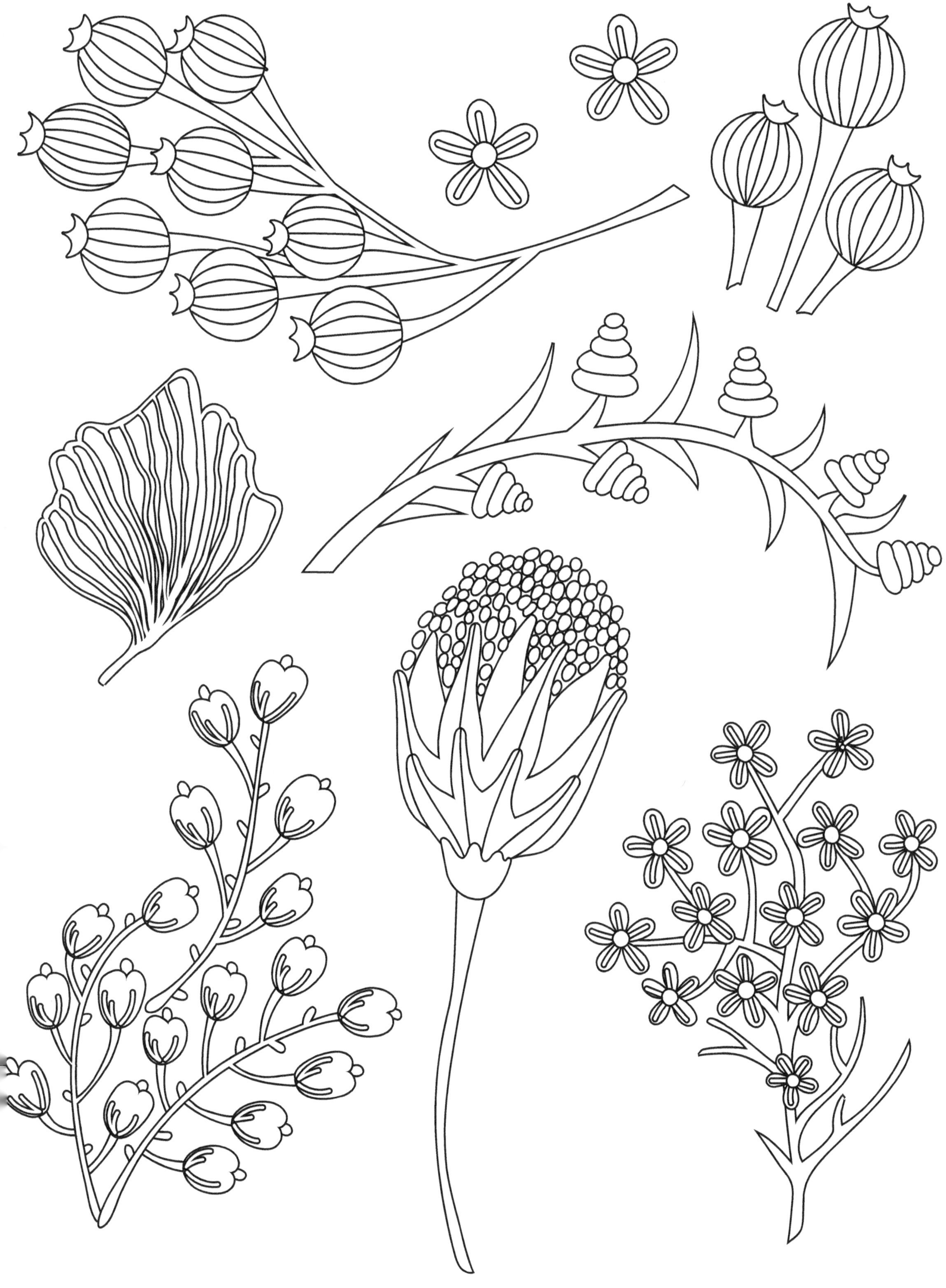

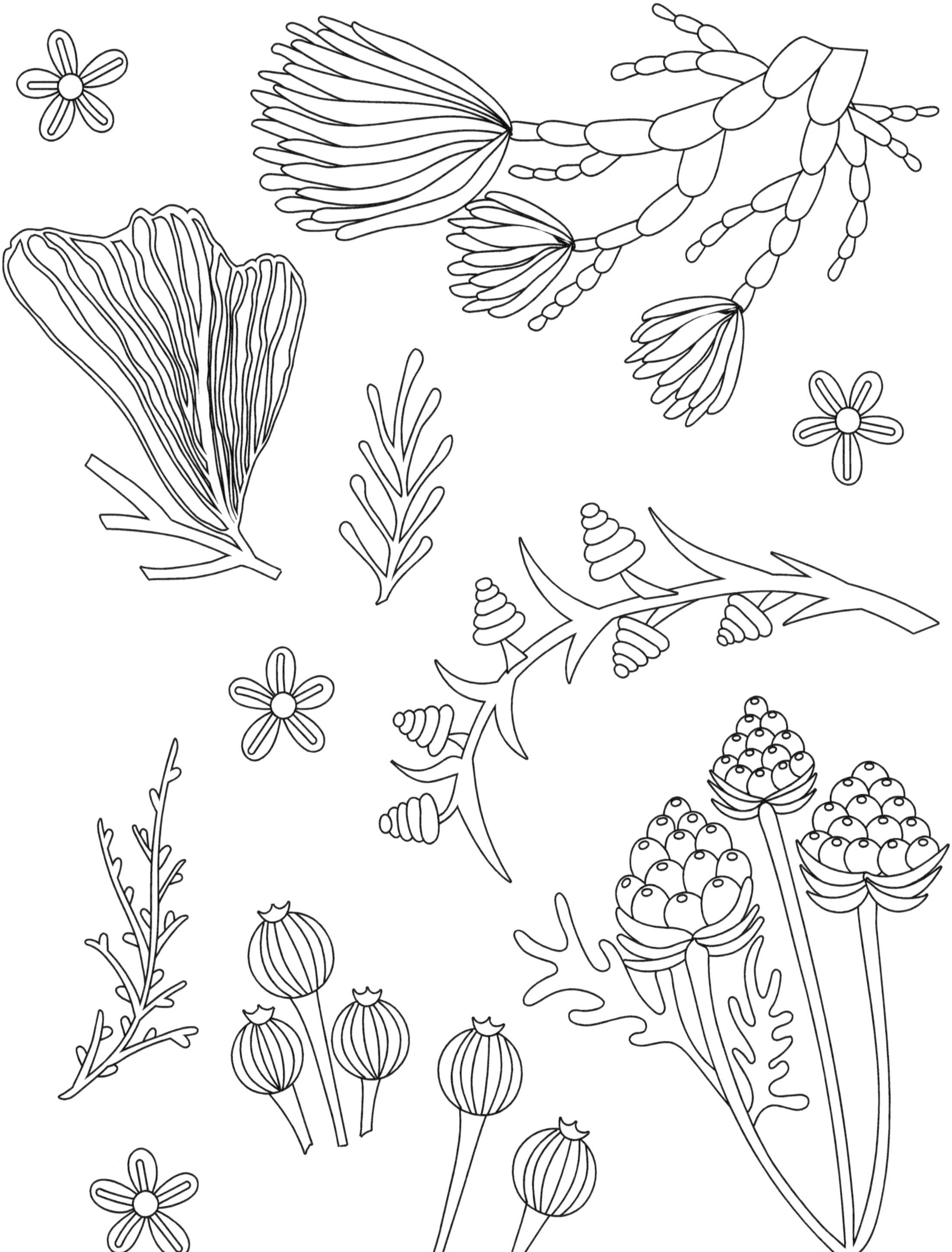

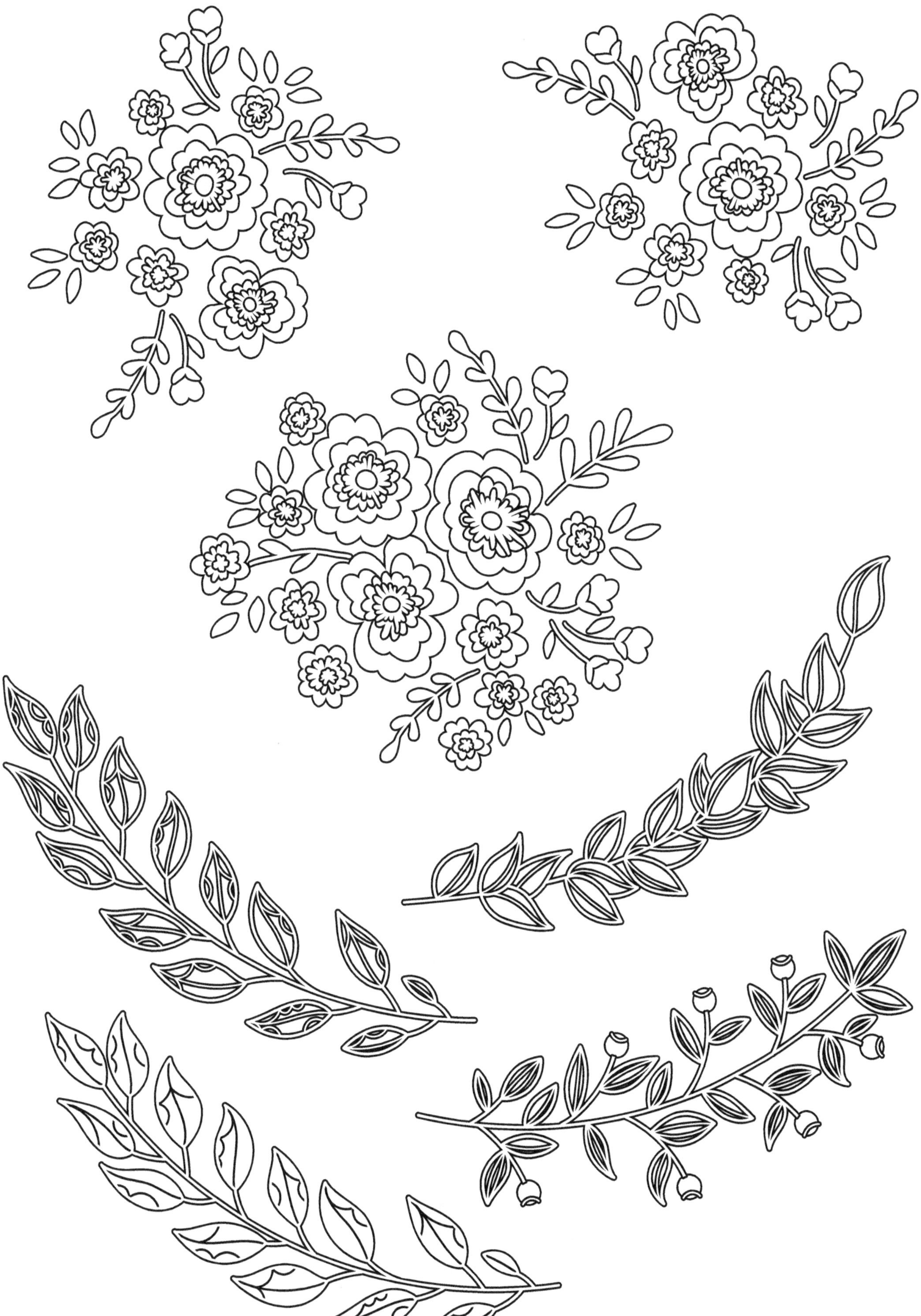

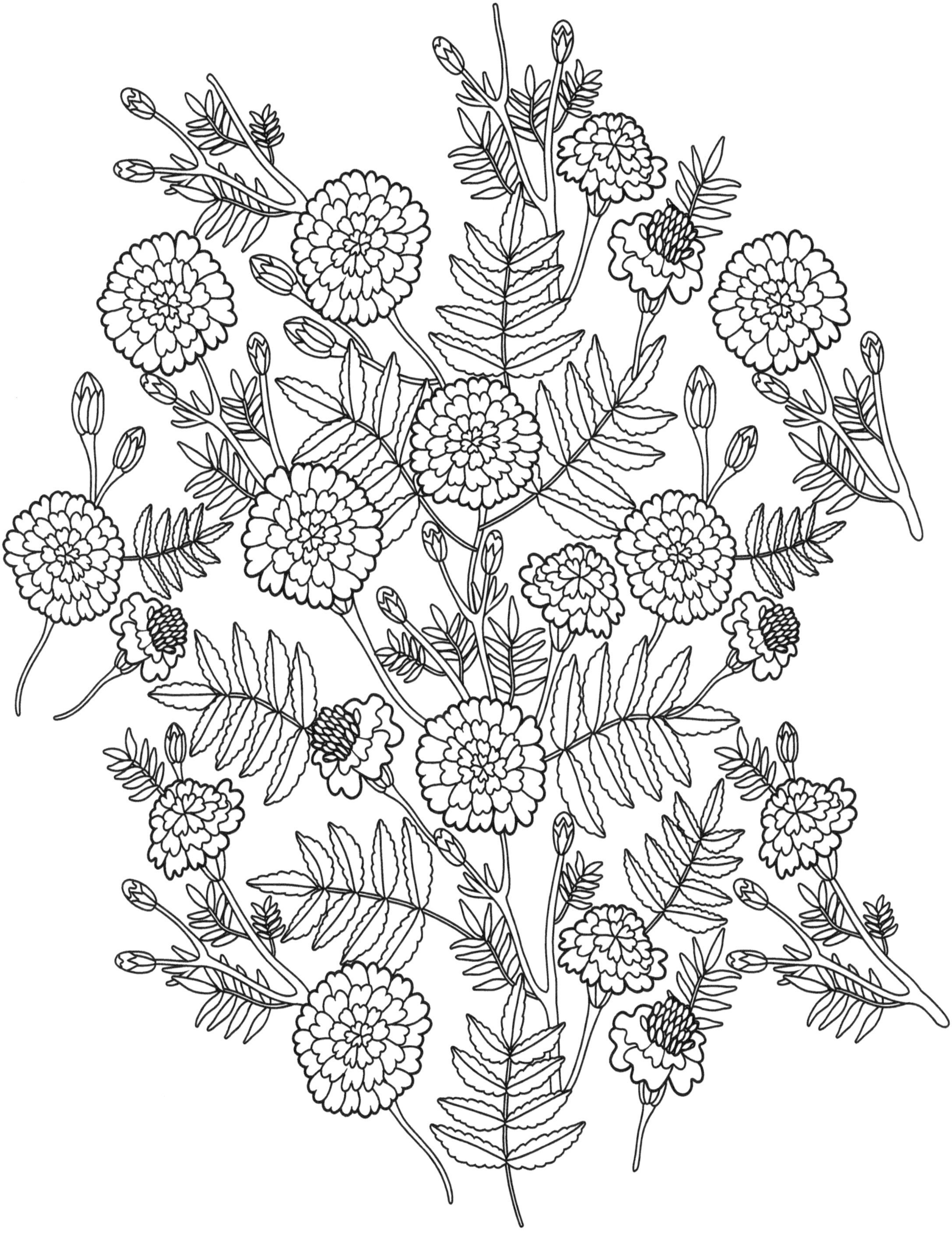

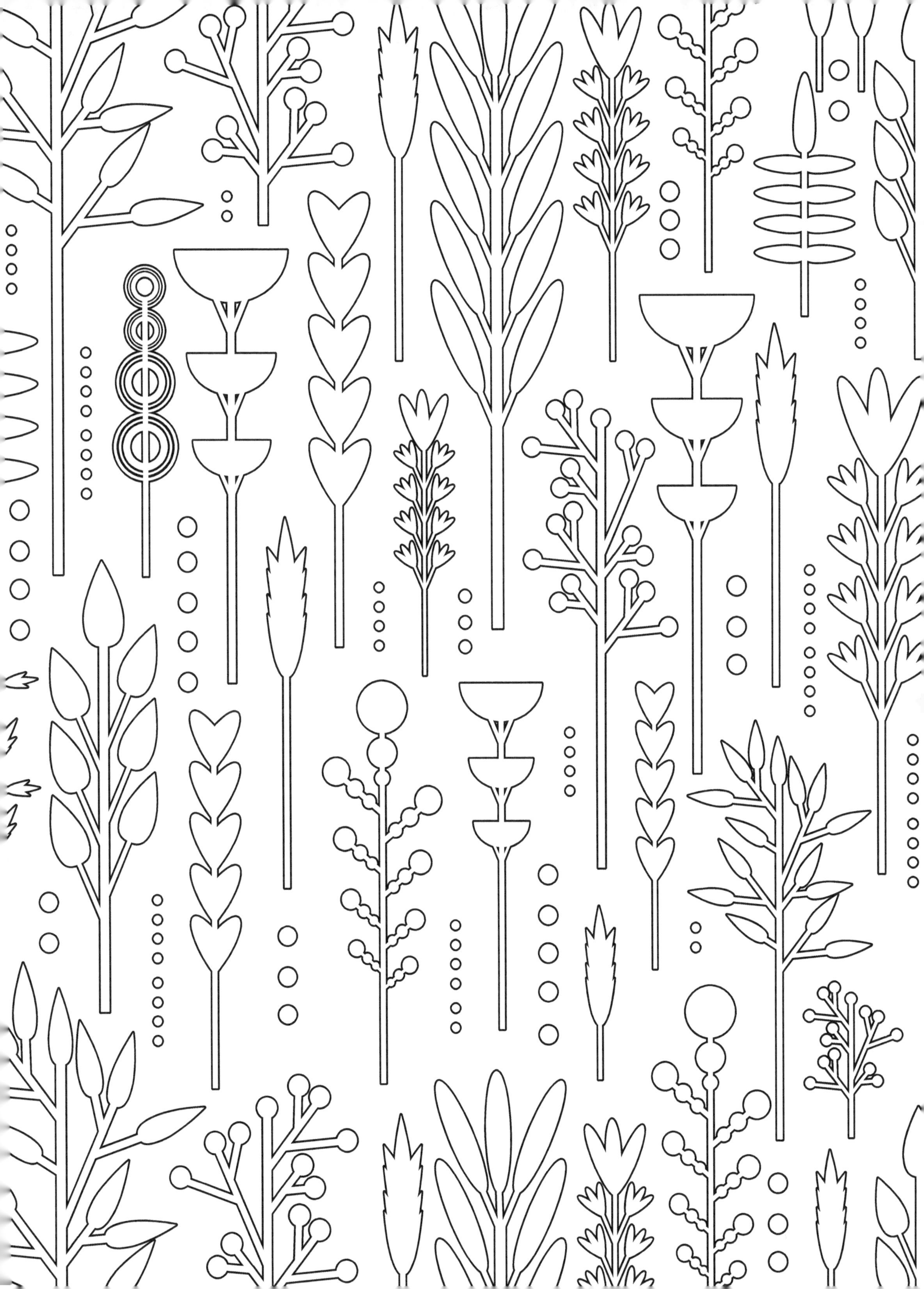

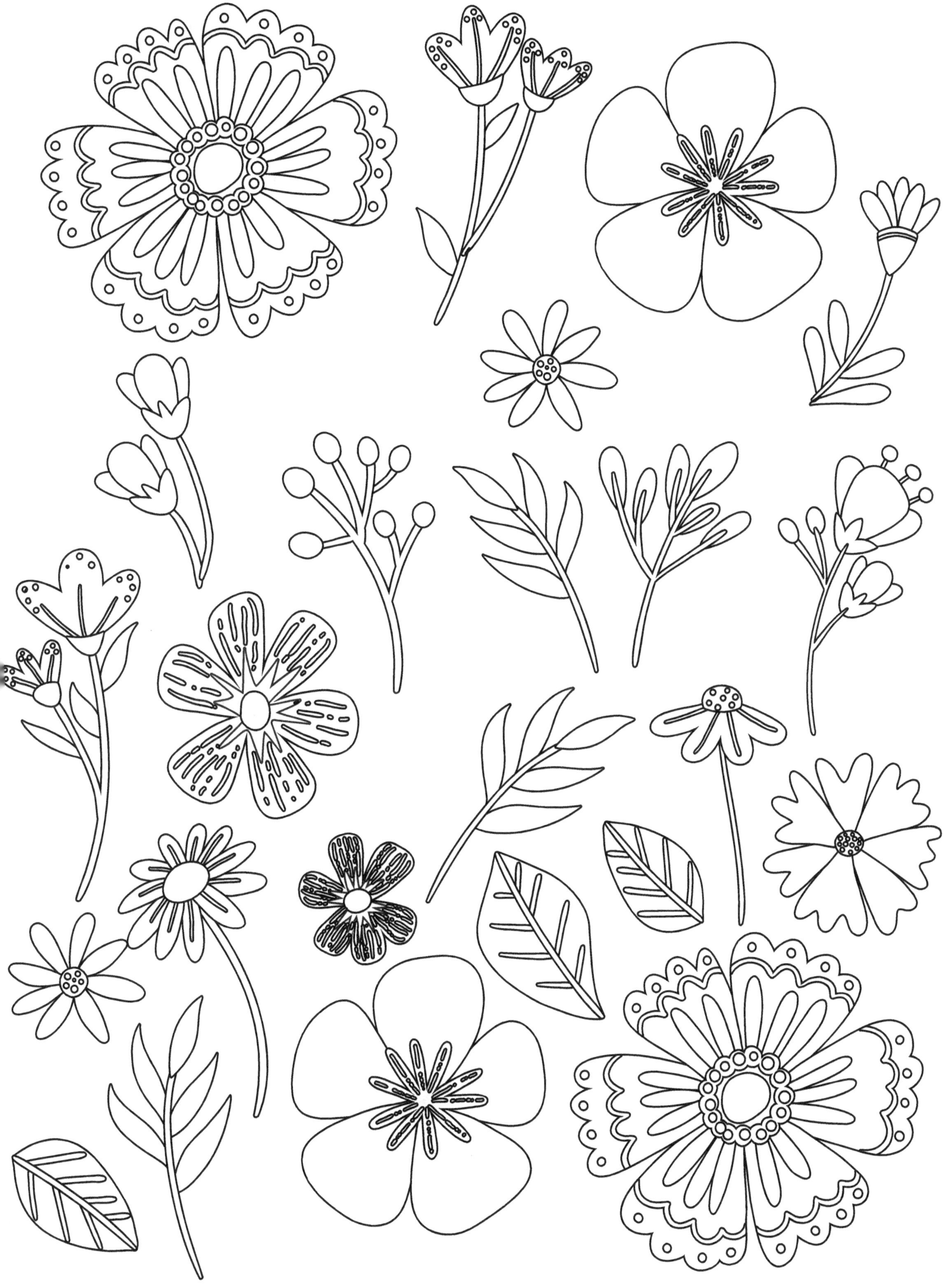

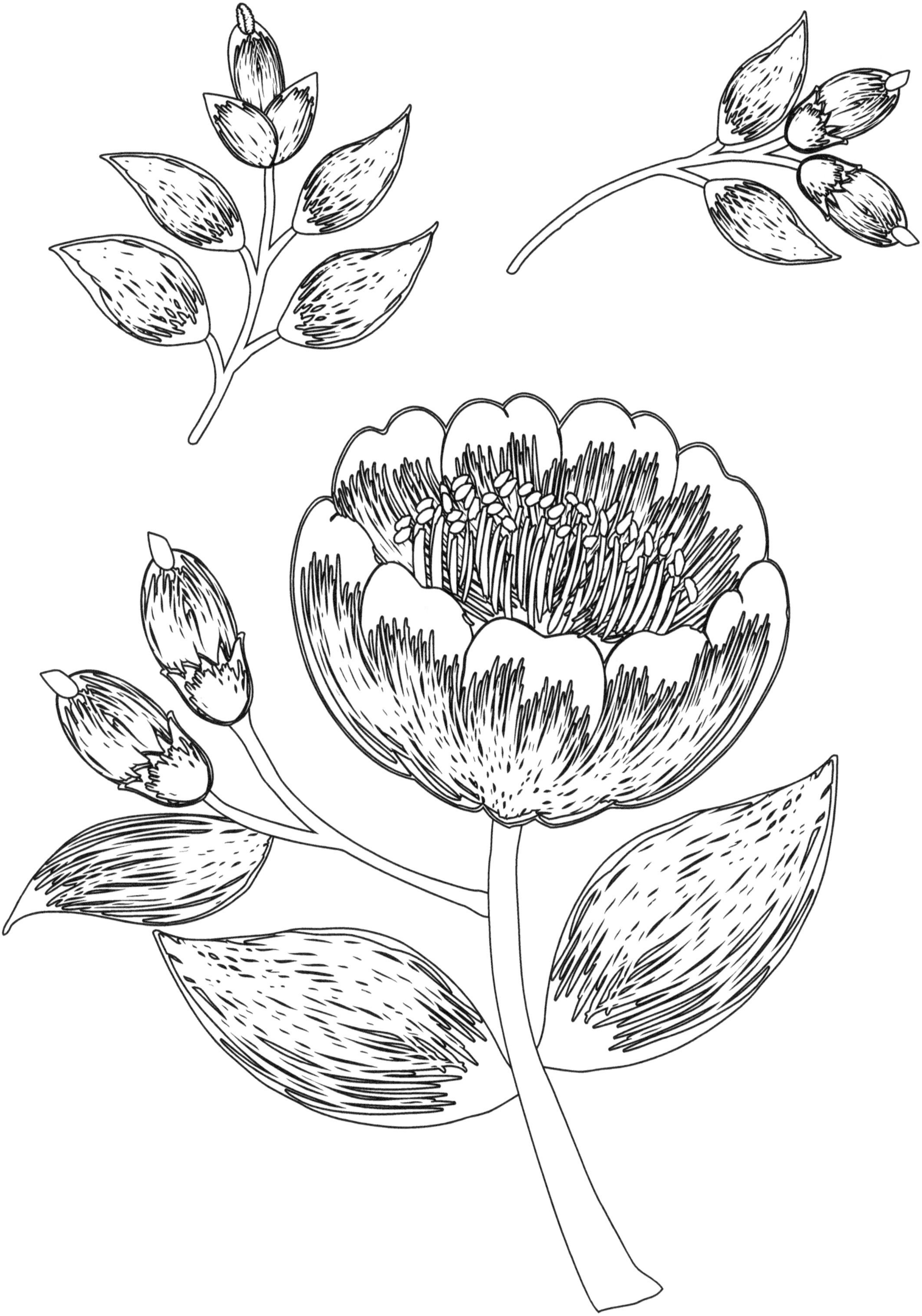

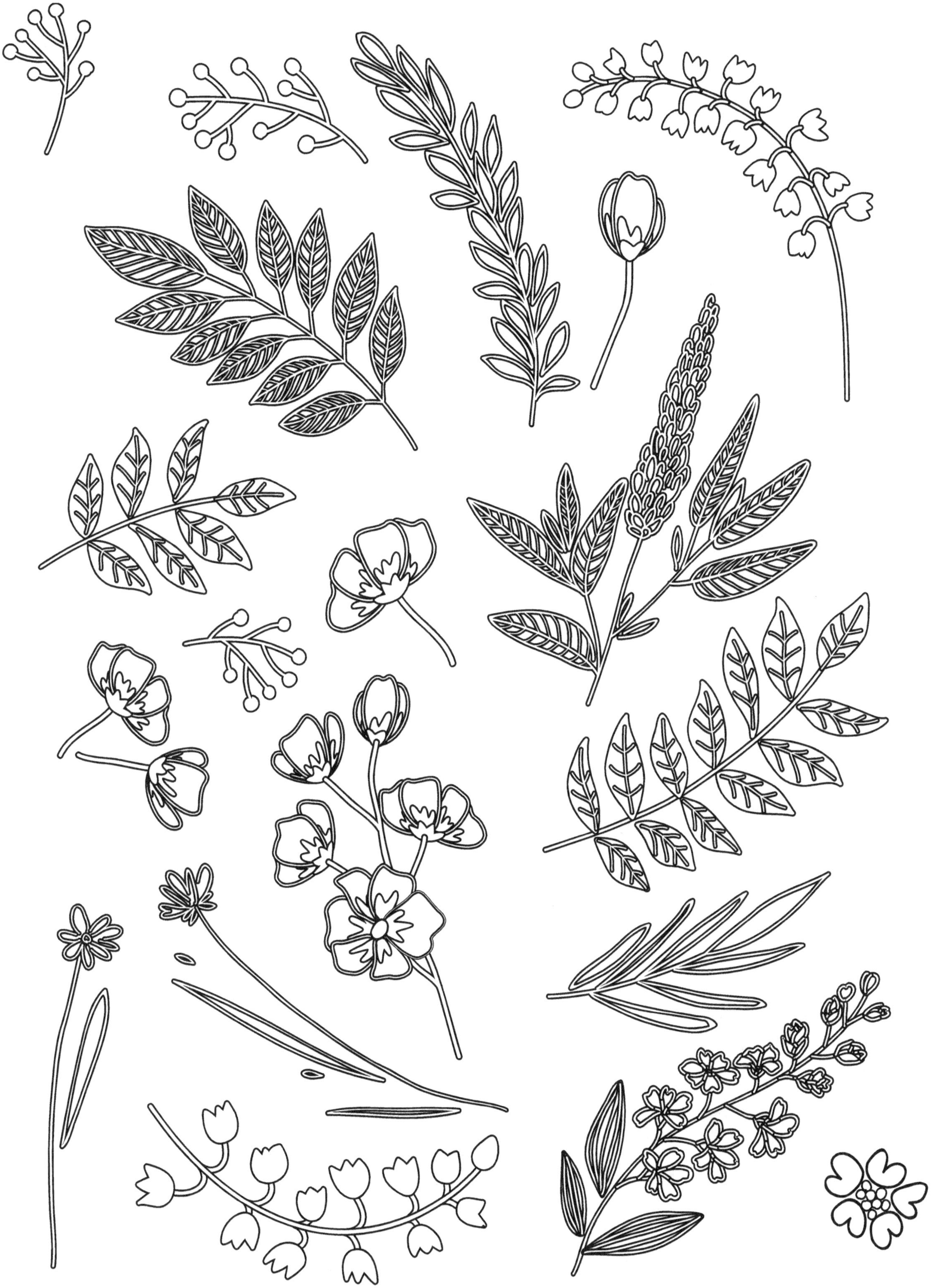

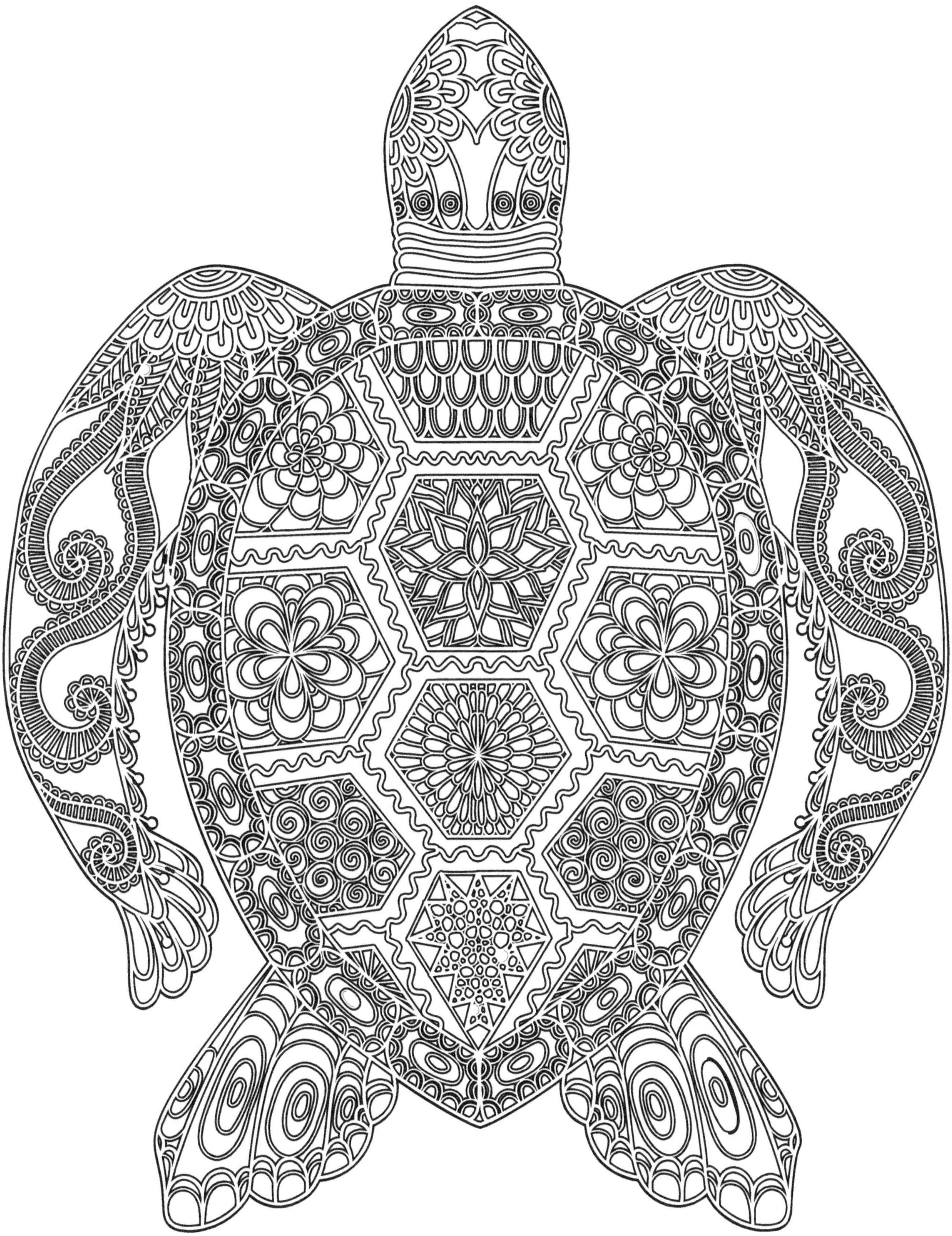

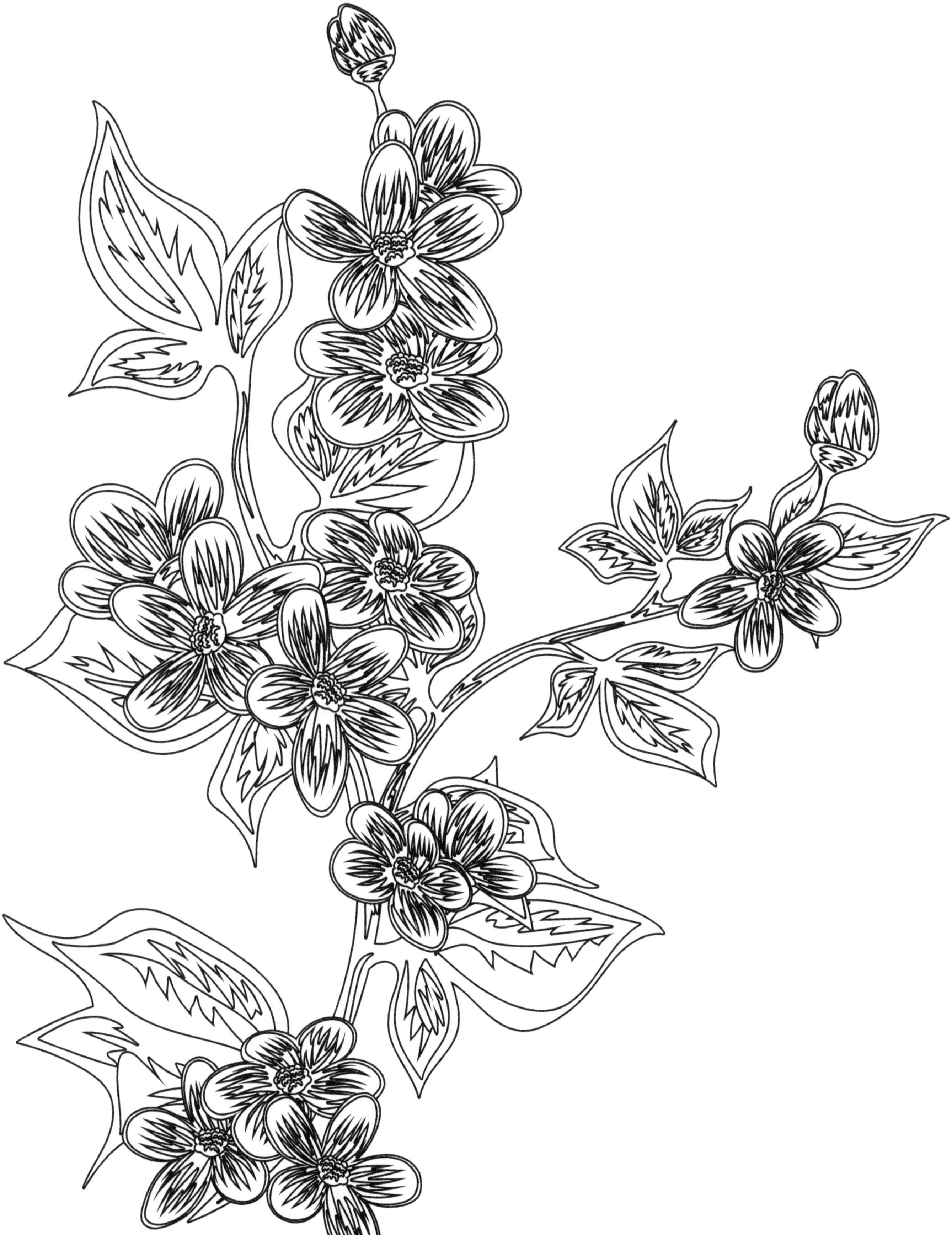

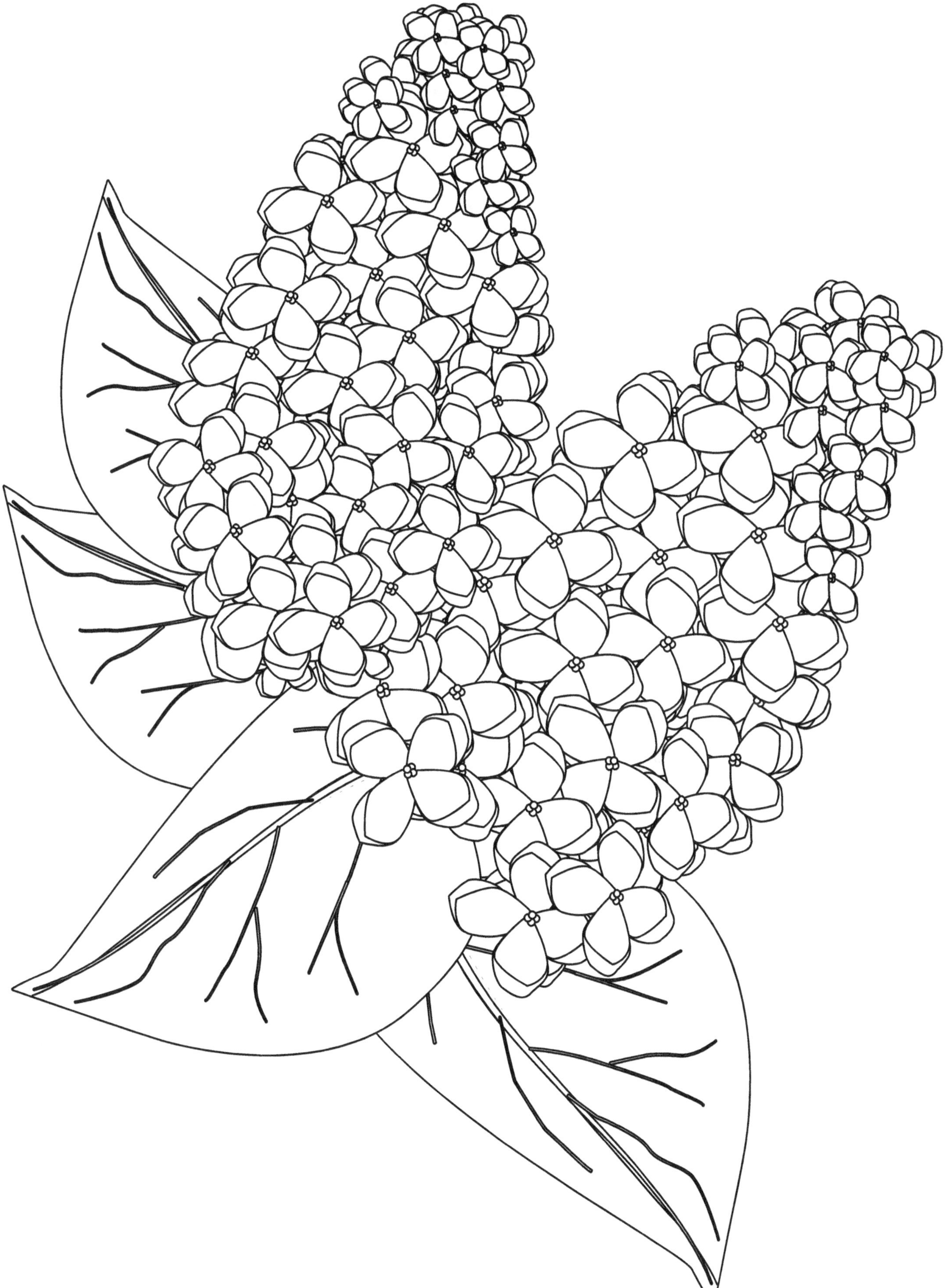

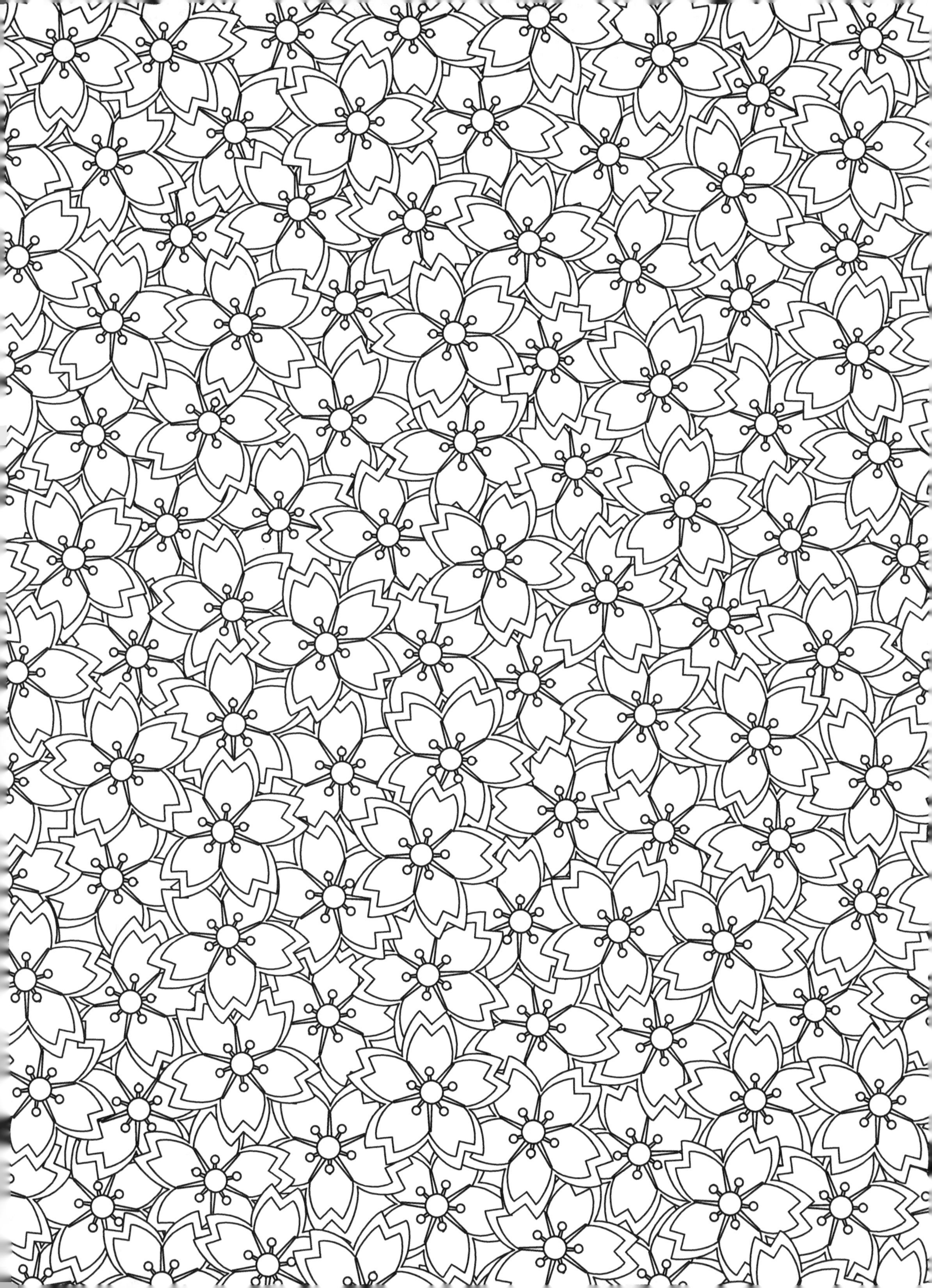

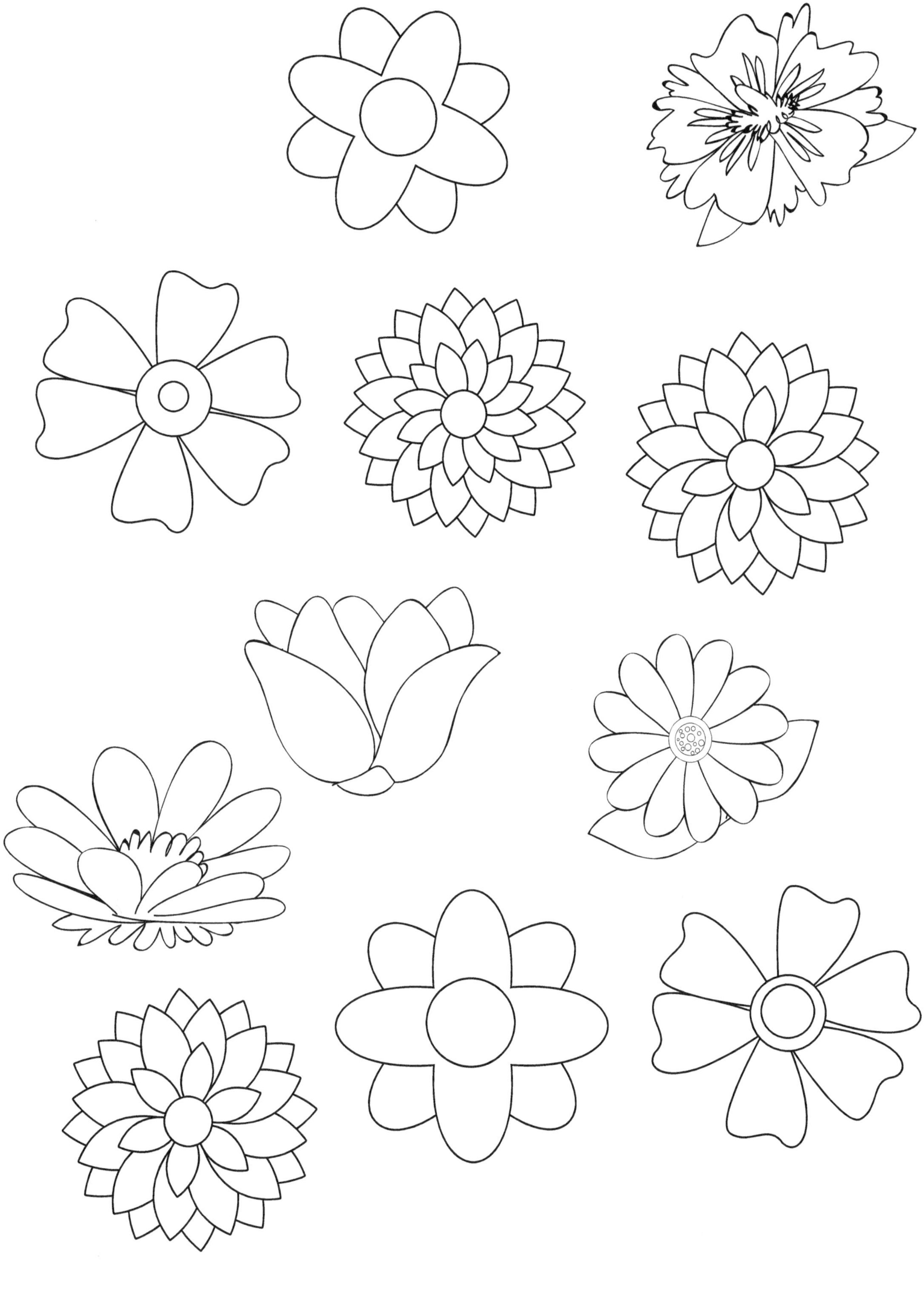

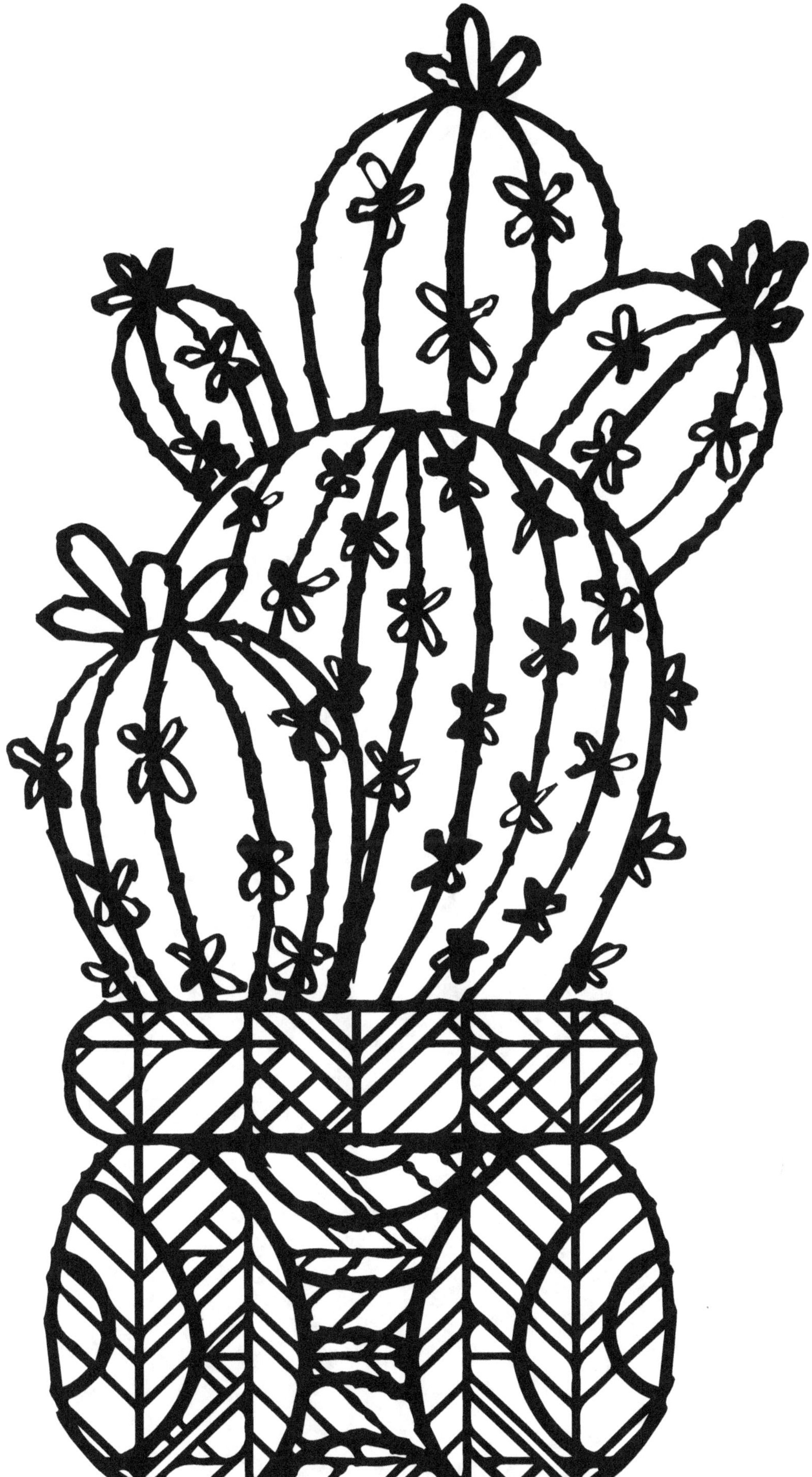

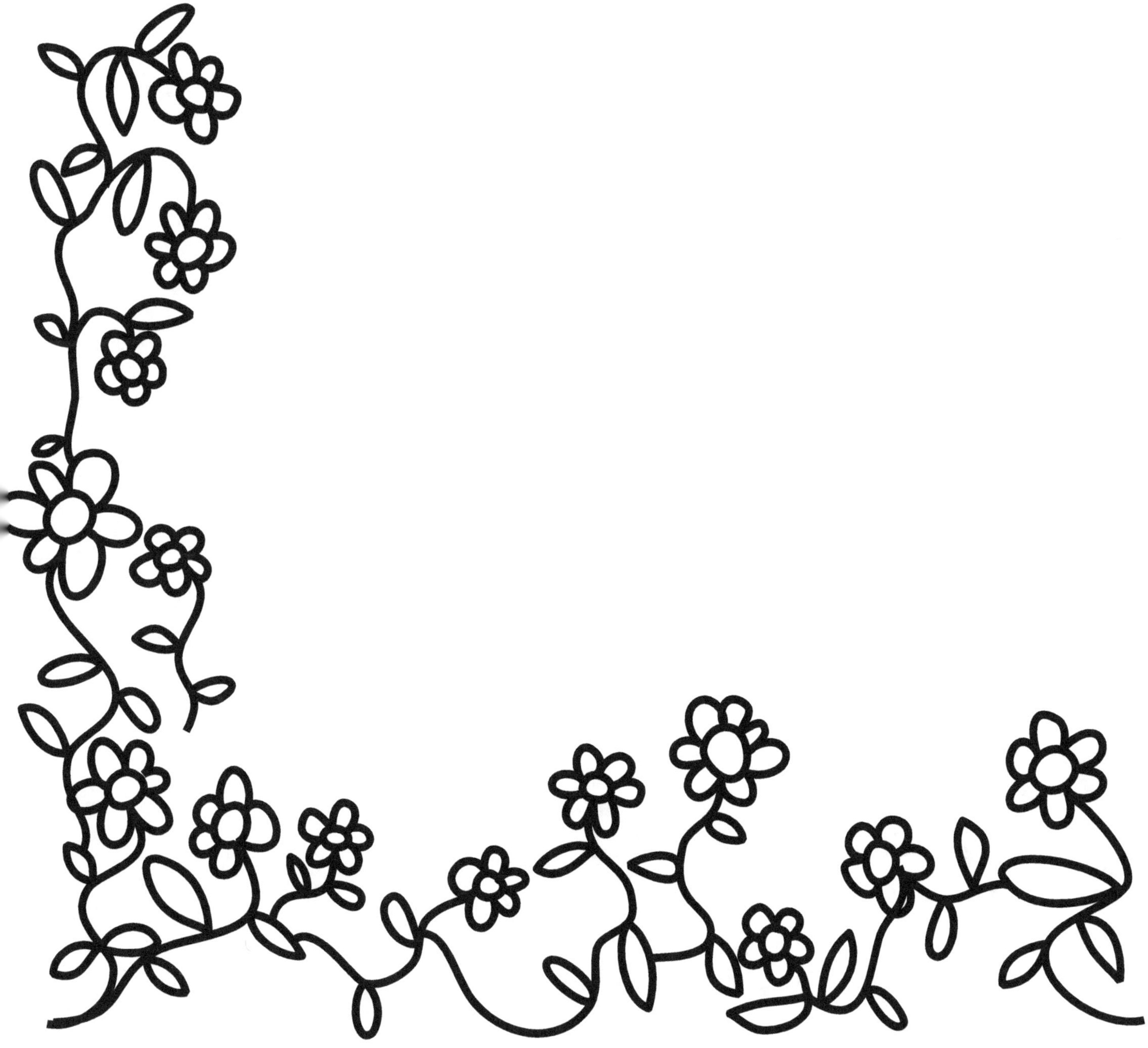

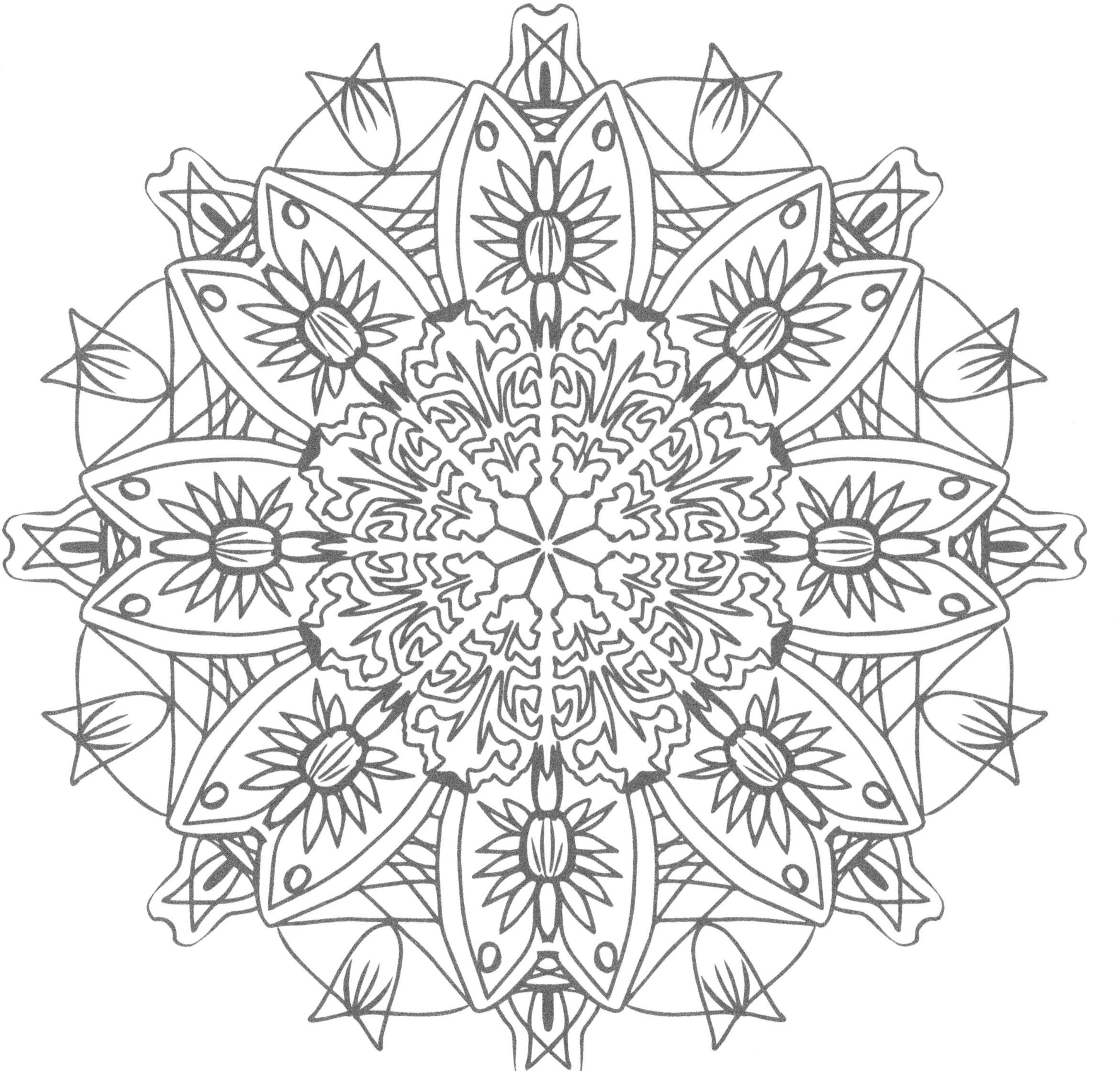

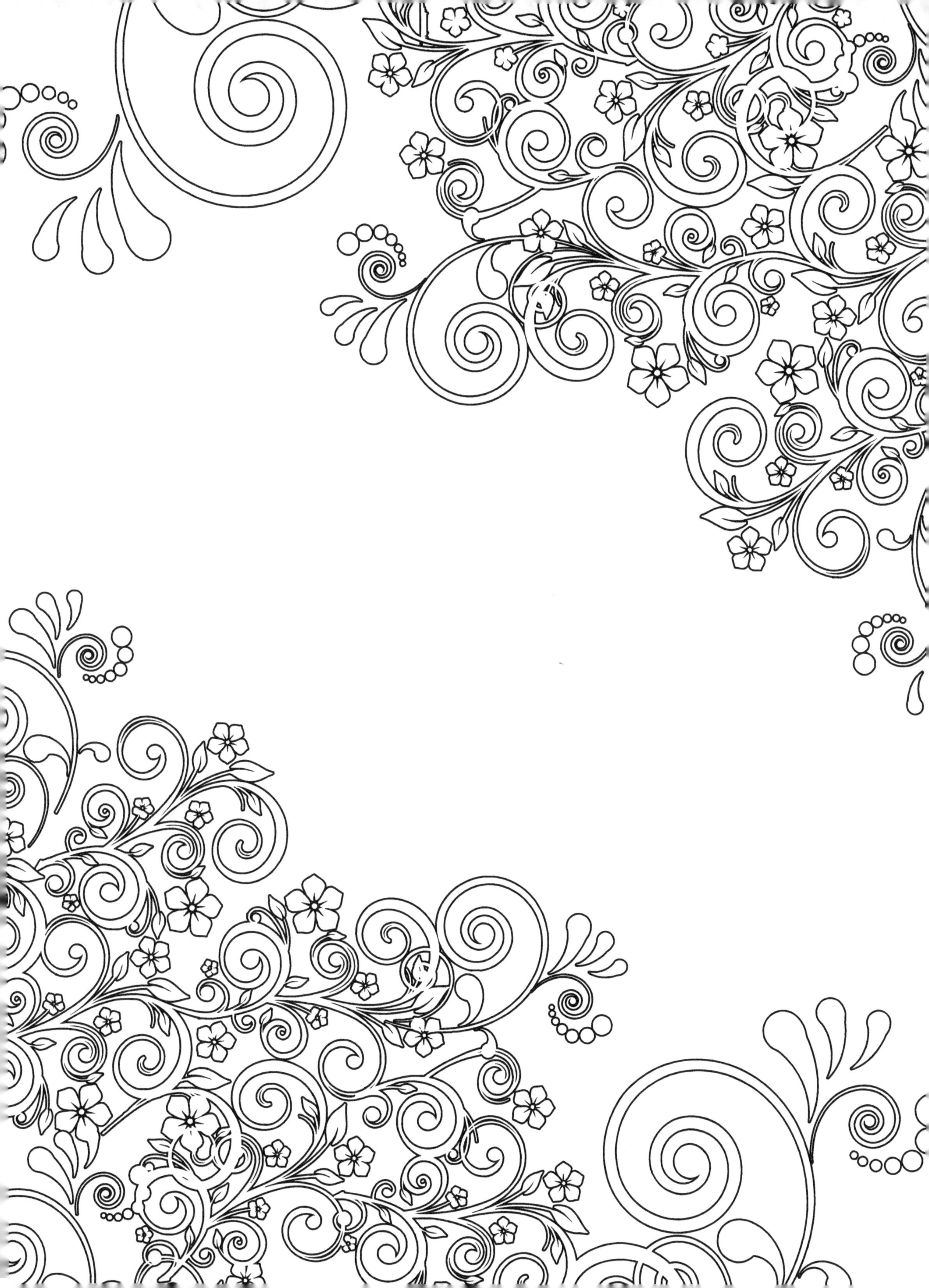

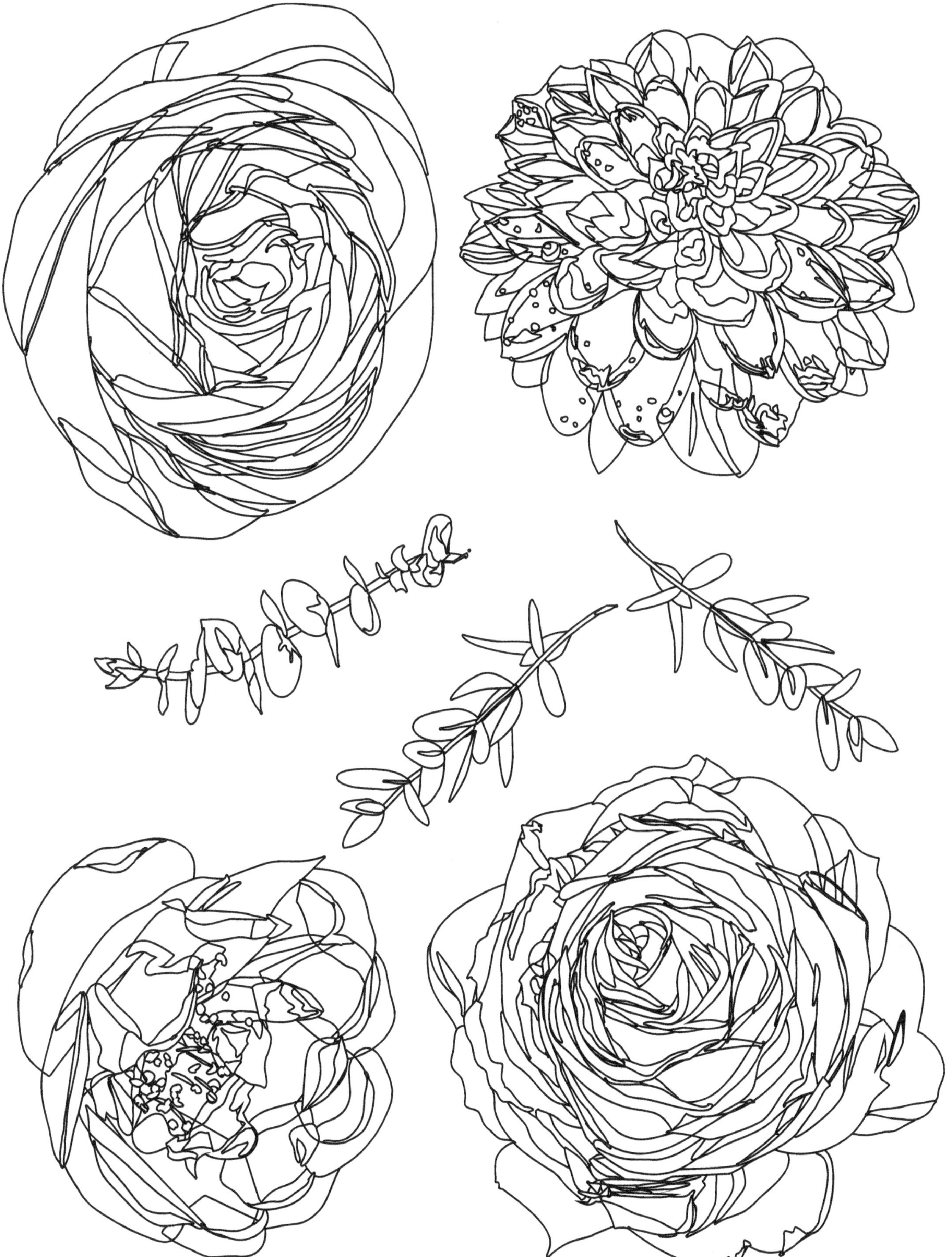

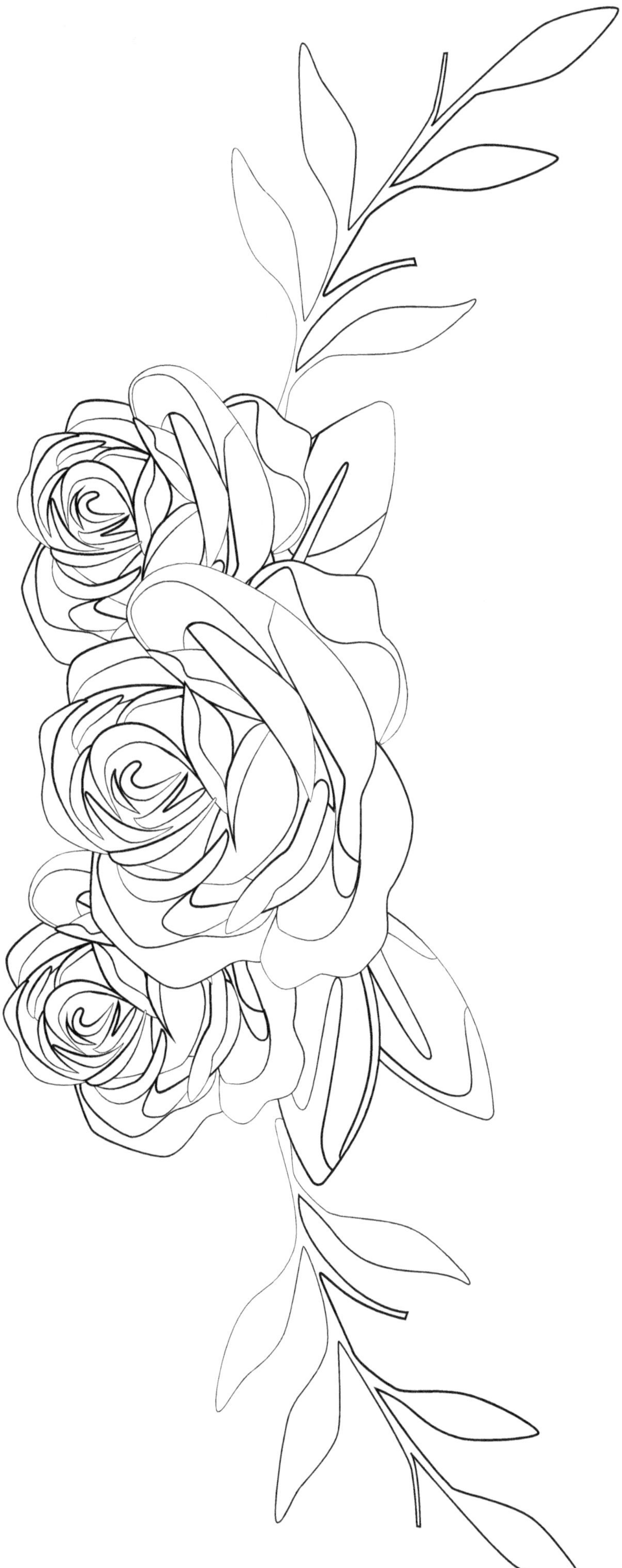

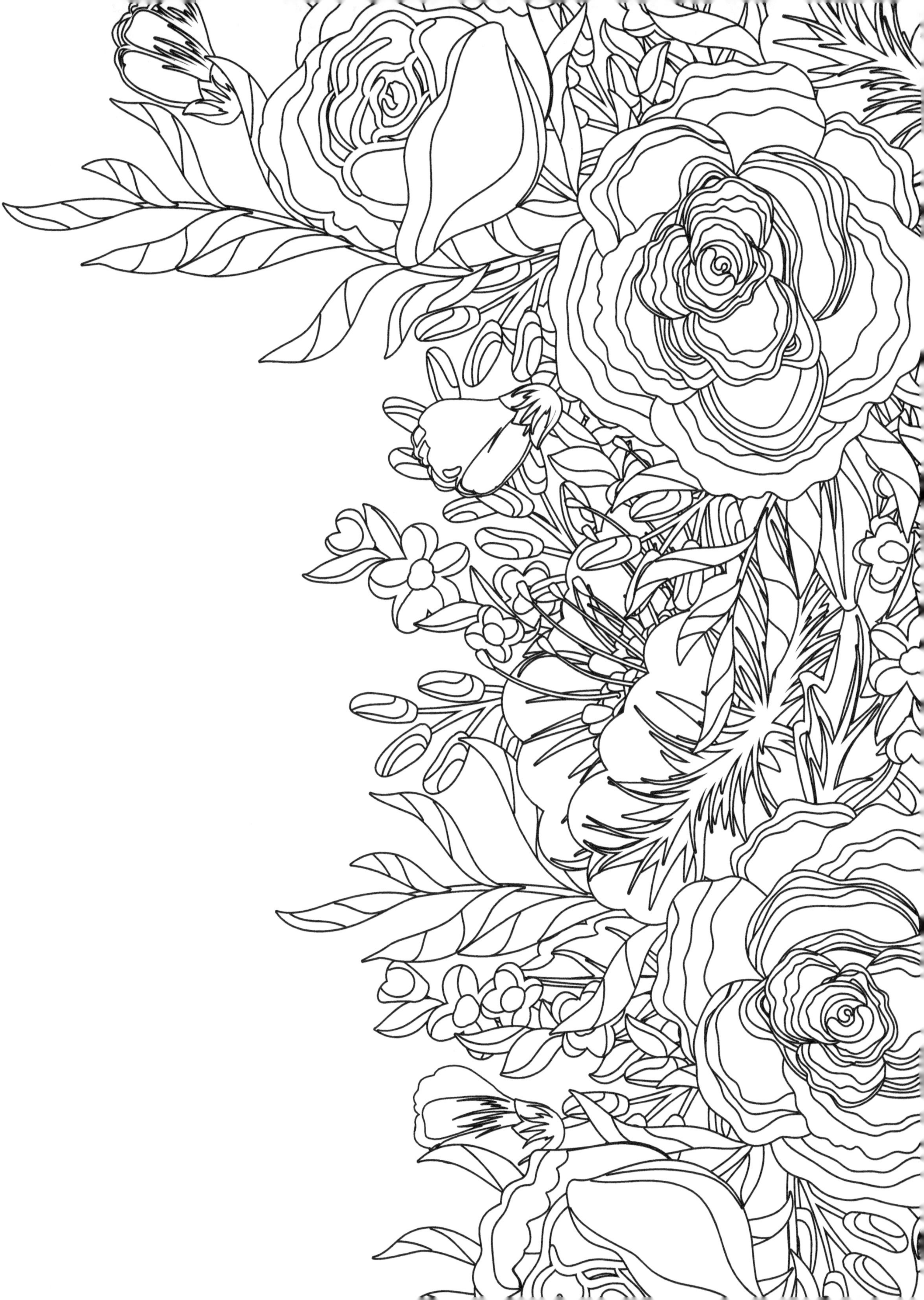

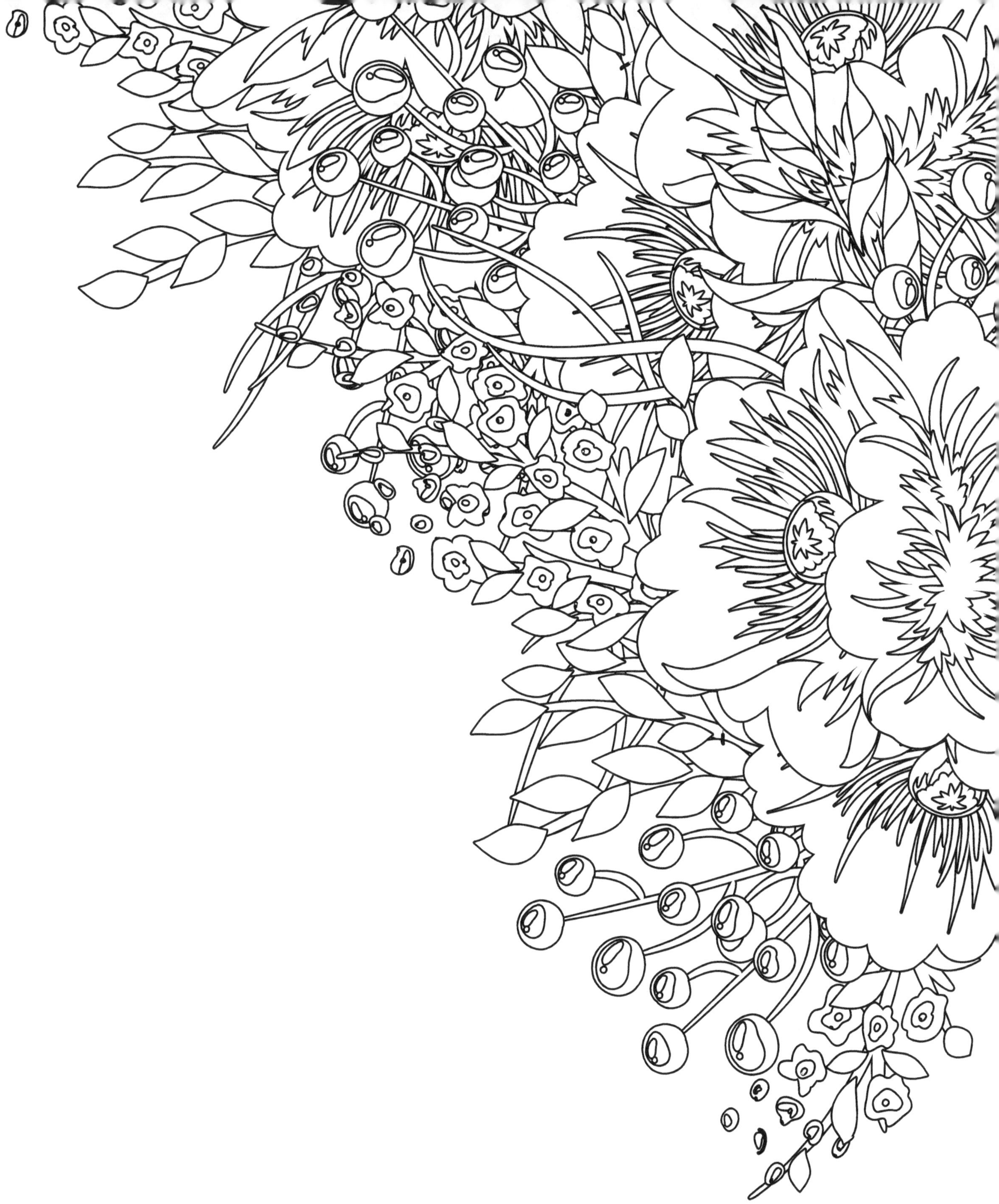

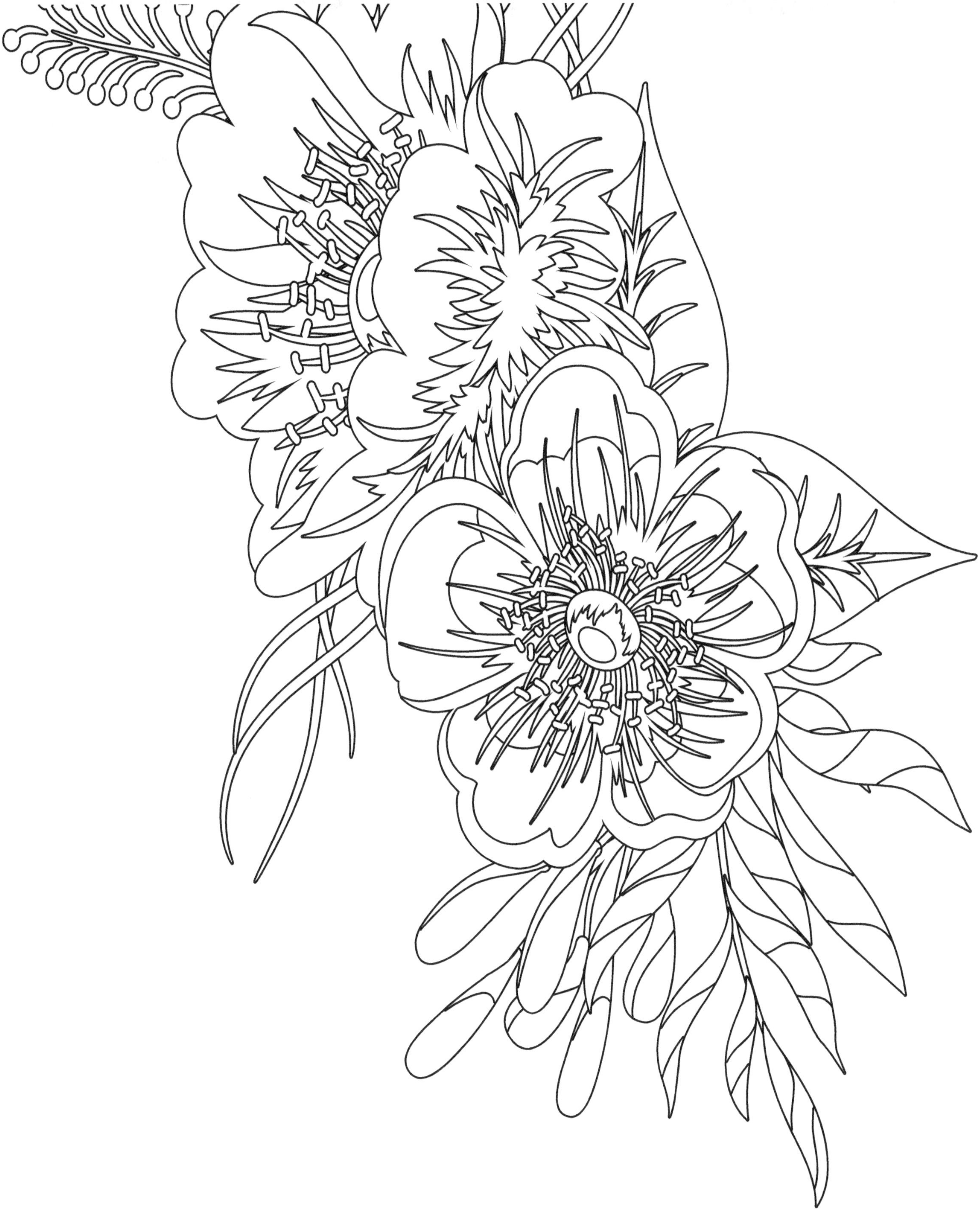

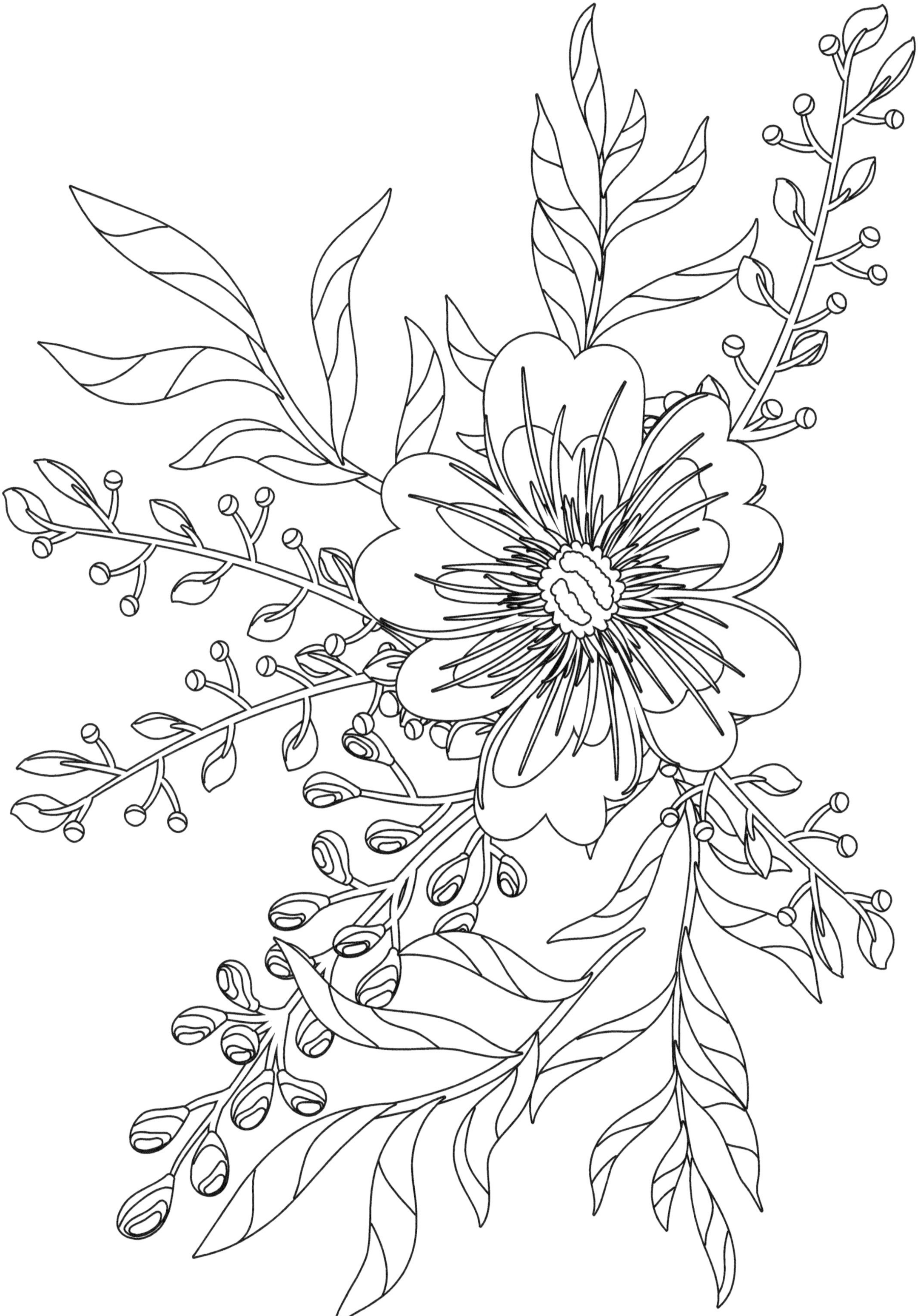

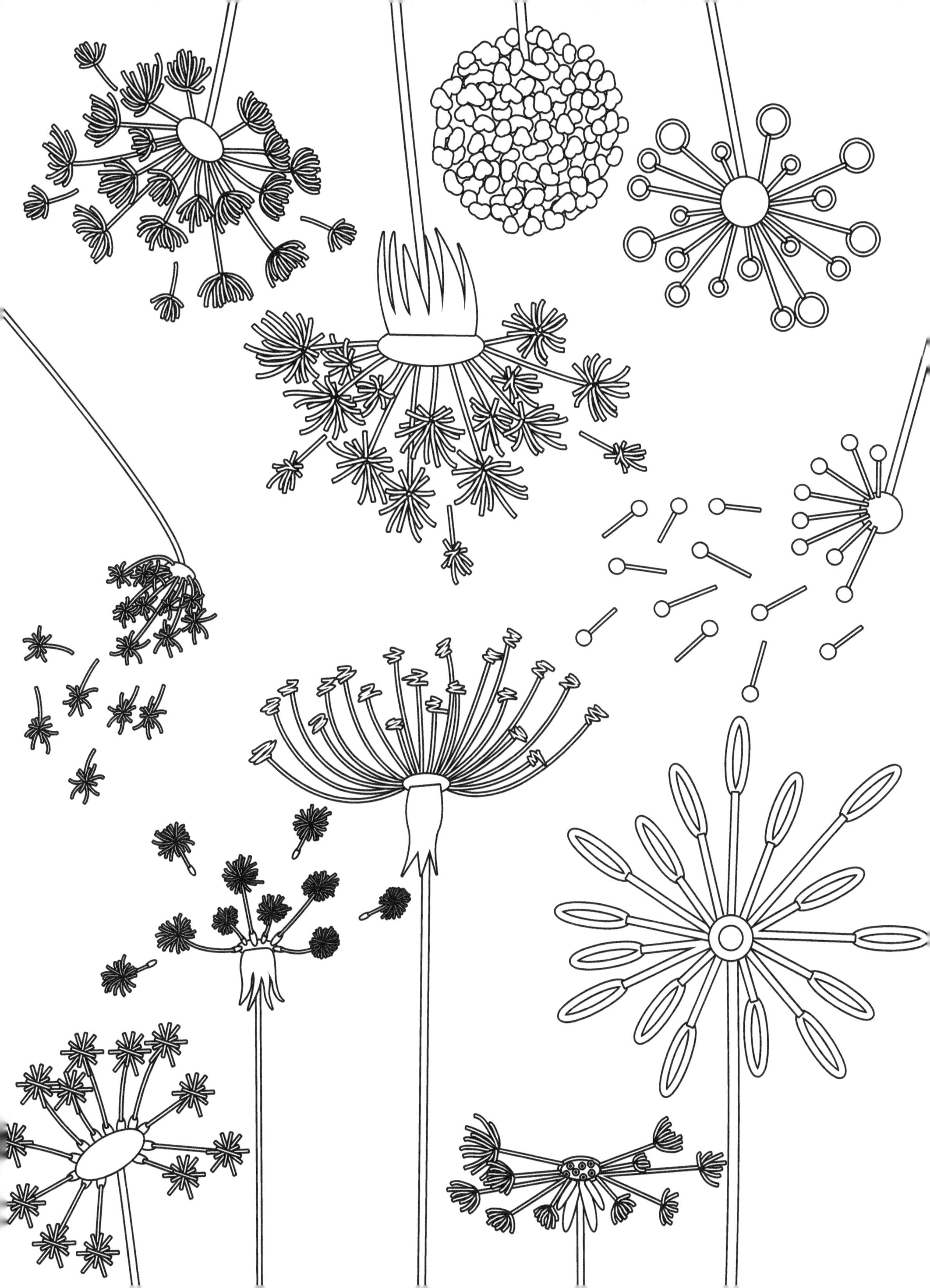

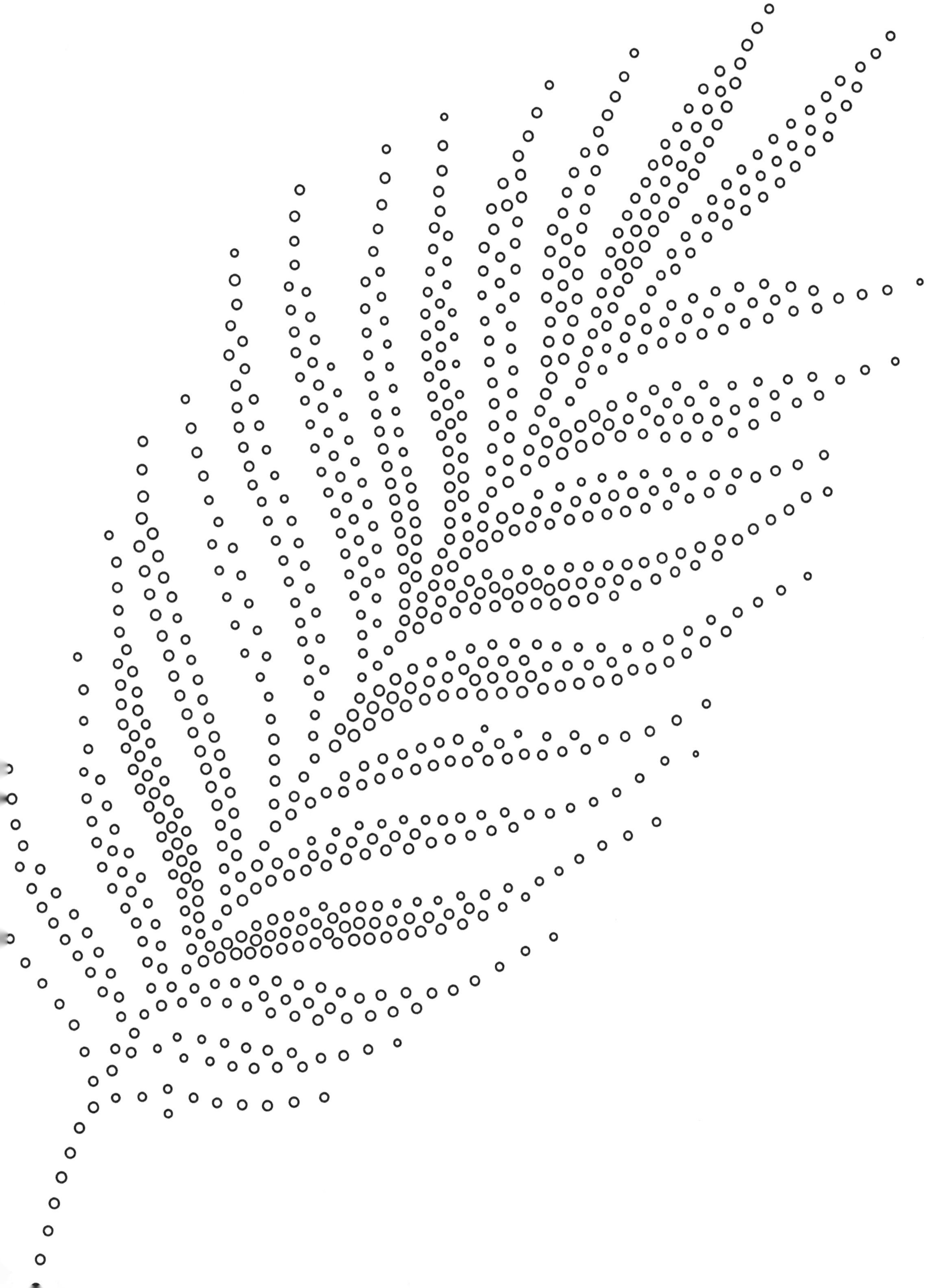

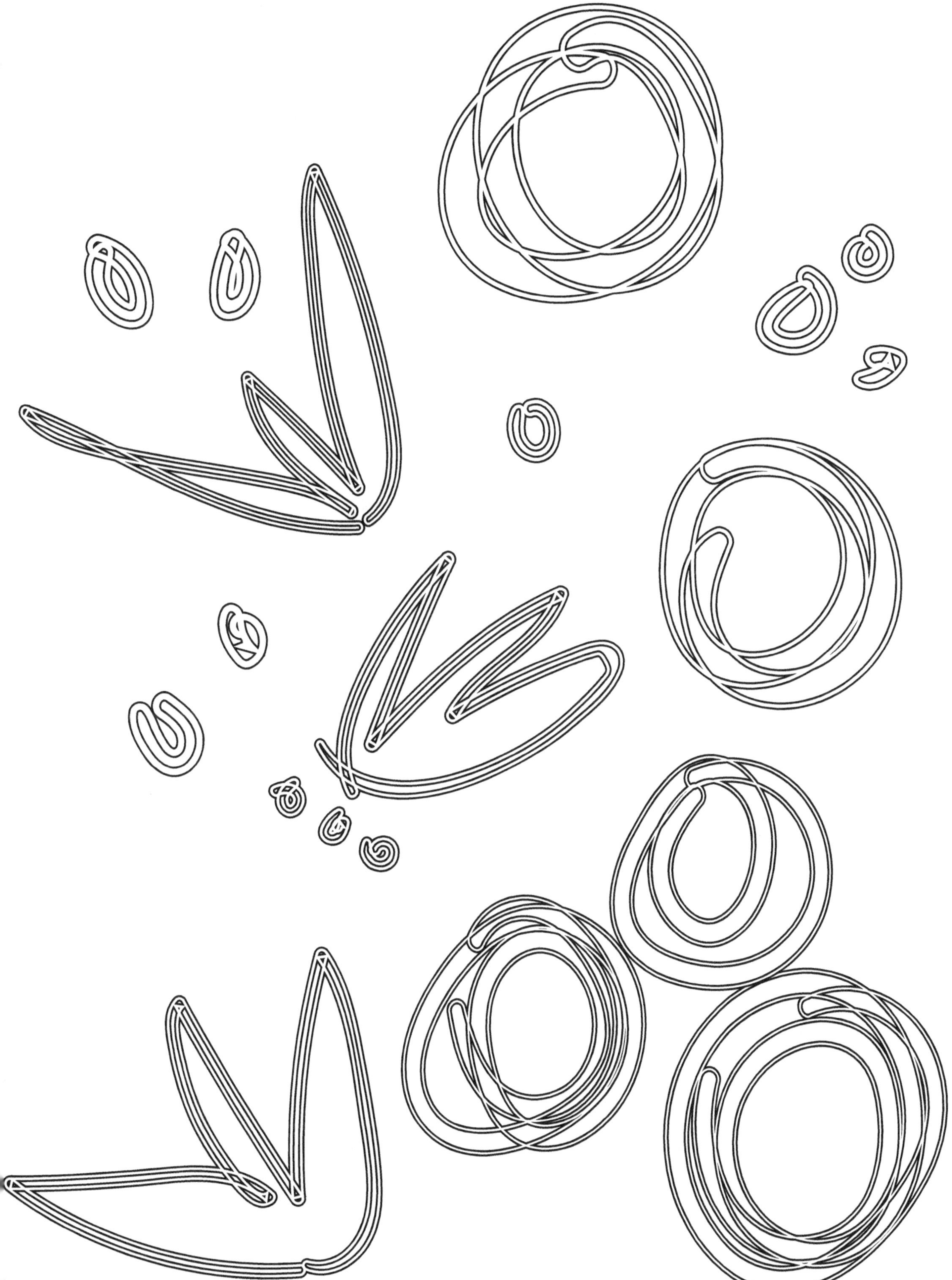

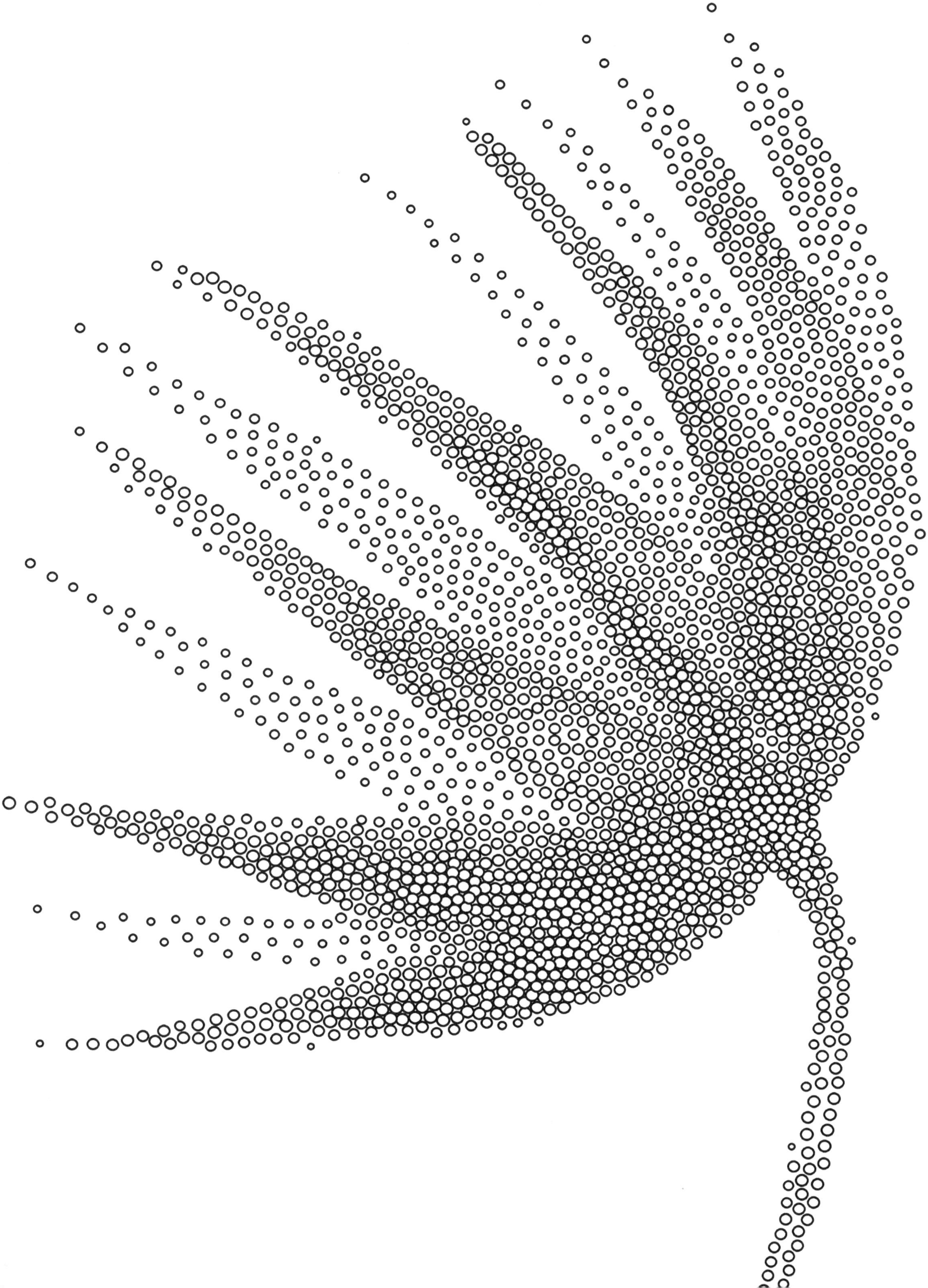

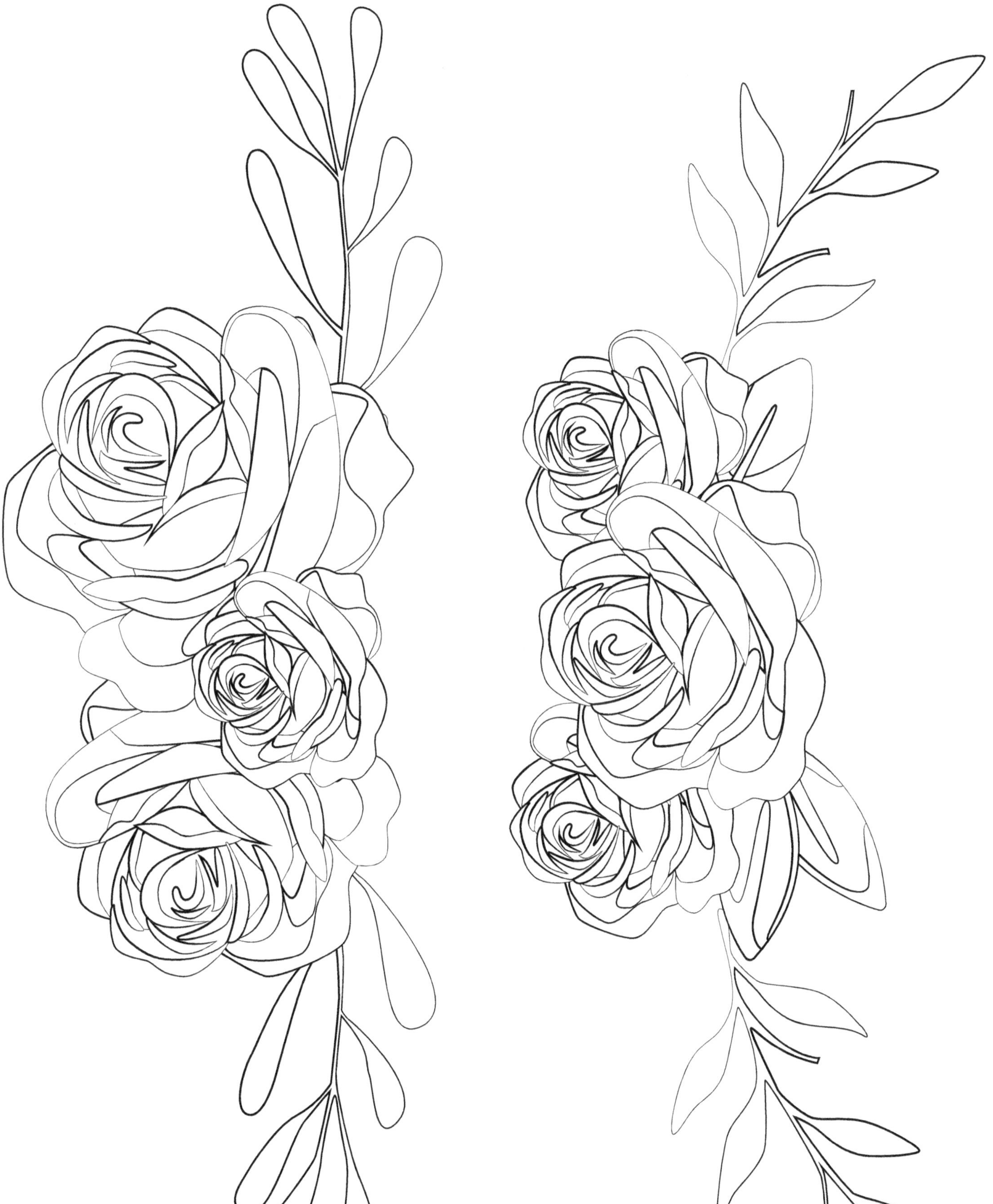

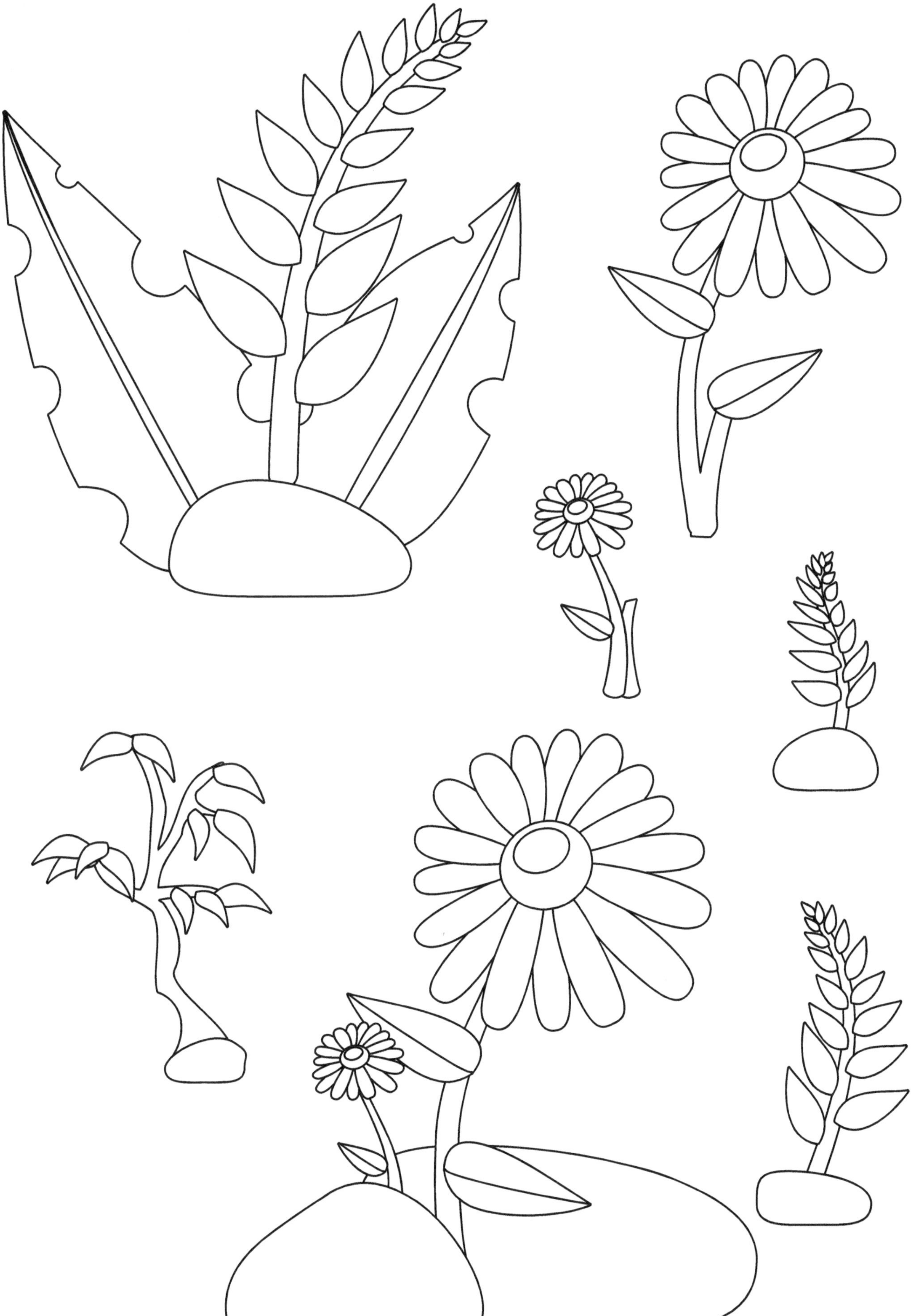

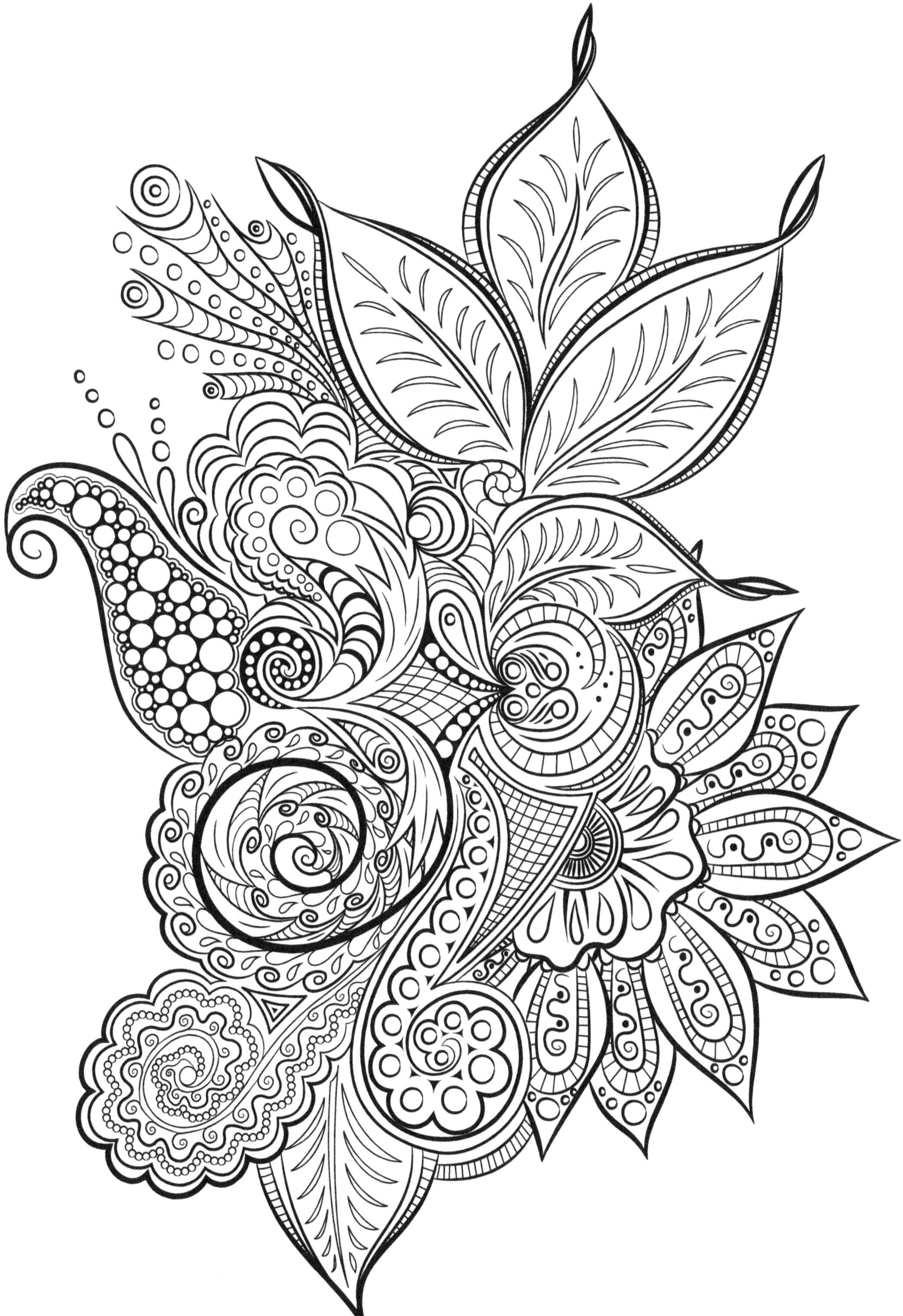

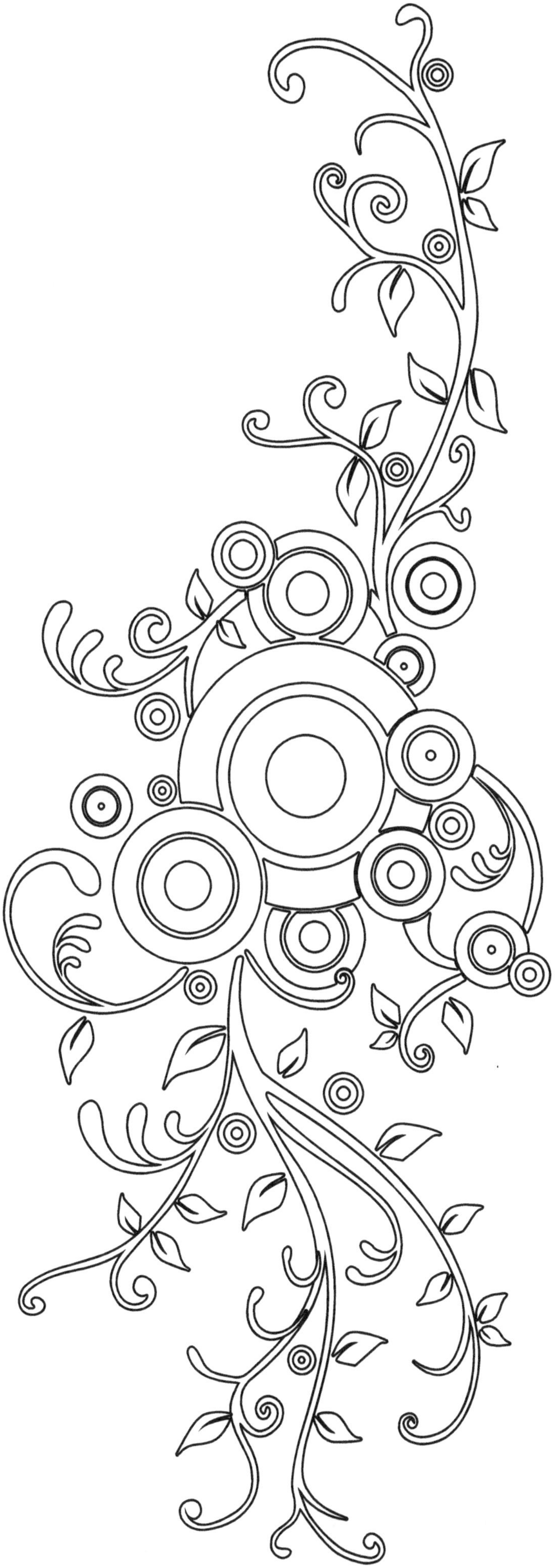

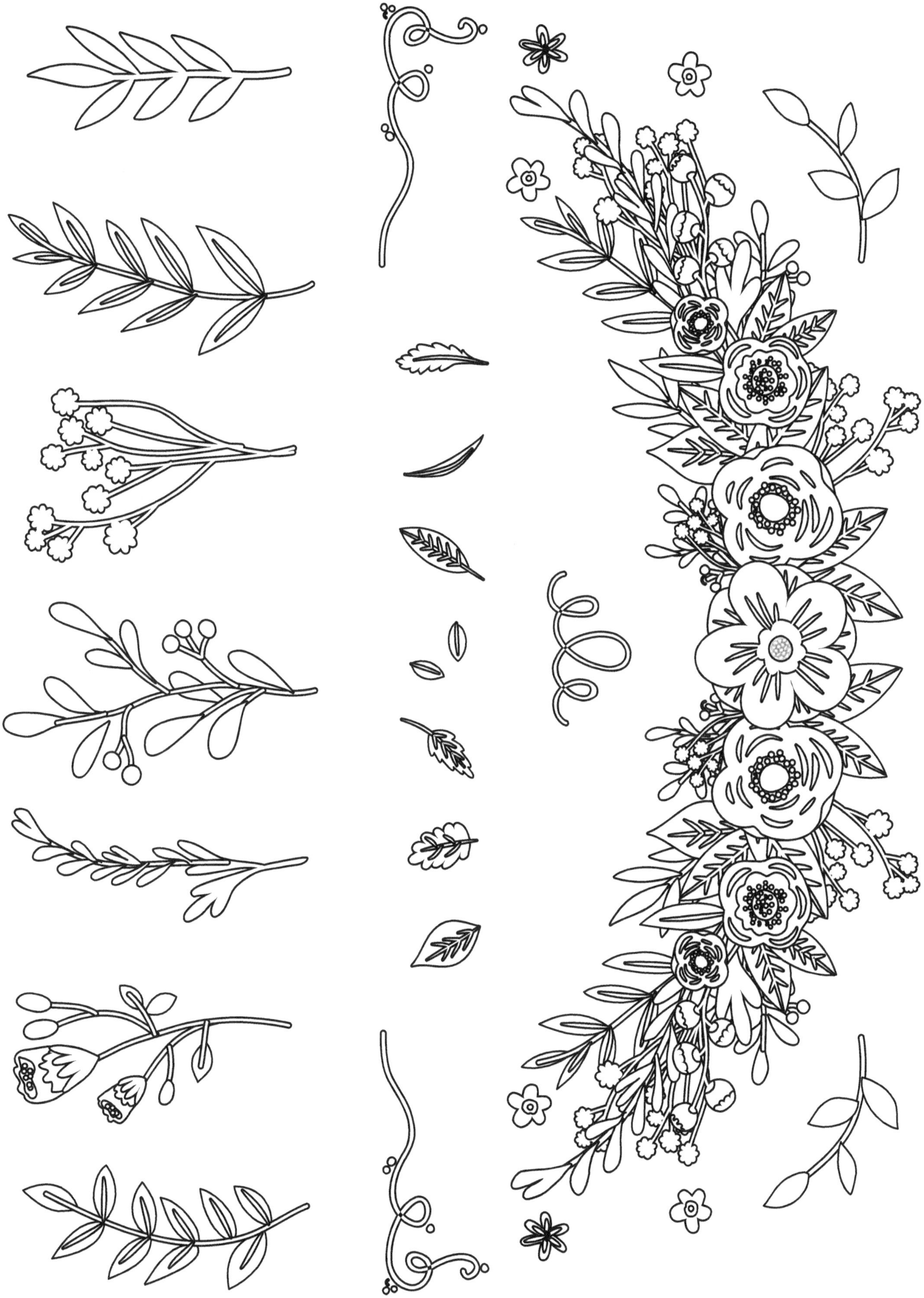

www.ingramcontent.com/pod-product-compliance
Lightning Source LLC
Chambersburg PA
CBHW081008170526
45158CB00010B/2964